It's another Quality Book from CGP

This book is for anyone doing GCSE English.

Whatever subject you're doing it's the same
old story — there are lots of facts and you've just got
to learn them. GCSE English is no different.

Happily this CGP book gives you all that important
information as clearly and concisely as possible.

It's also got some daft bits in to try and make the whole
experience at least vaguely entertaining for you.

What CGP is all about

Our sole aim here at CGP is to produce the highest quality
books — carefully written, immaculately presented and
dangerously close to being funny.

Then we work our socks off to get them out to you
— at the cheapest possible prices.

CONTENTS

Section Seven — Inform, Explain, Describe

Section Eight — Original Writing

Section Nine — Media and Non-Fiction Questions

Section Ten — Language & Grammar

Section Eleven — Speaking & Listening

Published by Coordination Group Publications Ltd.

Contributors:
Taissa Csaky
Chris Dennett
Dominic Hall
Kerry Kolbe
Tim Major
Becky May
Katherine Reed
Chrissy Williams

ISBN: 978 1 84146 101 4

Groovy website: www.cgpbooks.co.uk
Jolly bits of clipart from CorelDRAW®
Printed by Elanders Hindson Ltd, Newcastle upon Tyne.

What You Have to Do

GCSE English exams — yep, they're on their way. But they're <u>not</u> as scary as you think. Honest... Anyway, fasten your seat belts and hold on tight because <u>we're going in</u>...

You'll Have to Do <u>Lots</u> of Different <u>Things</u>

English exams are funny ones — there are loads of different parts to the exam, so you need lots of different skills to do well overall. Here's a break-down of what you'll have to do:

The Scary Bits — <u>Under</u> Exam Conditions

This is the 'meat' of the exams — clock ticking, heart palpitations-type stuff.

1) **LITERATURE ESSAYS** — Answer questions about the <u>poetry</u>, <u>prose</u> or <u>drama</u> that you've been studying in class. They could cover characters, style, tone, themes etc.

2) **EXPLAINING ESSAY** — <u>Explain</u>, or <u>describe</u> something to the reader, or <u>inform</u> them about something.

3) **ARGUING ESSAY** — <u>Argue</u> a particular point and <u>persuade</u> readers to agree with a point of view, or <u>advise</u> readers about something. It needs strong persuasive writing skills.

4) **DIFFERENT CULTURES** — Write about poems or short stories by writers from outside the UK.

5) **RESPONDING TO UNSEEN TEXTS** — <u>Read</u> a piece of text in the exam (often a magazine or newspaper article) and then answer questions in <u>response</u> to it.

Slightly Less Scary — Coursework

There shouldn't be any sweaty-palm moments here.

6) **LITERATURE ESSAYS** — Same as 1) — write essays about the <u>texts</u> you've studied in class. This time, though, you'll have loads more time to think about it and make it extra brilliant. One of them will have to be about a Shakespeare play.

7) **ANALYSING ESSAY** — <u>Analyse</u> and <u>comment</u> on something, or <u>review</u> something. (Some exam boards do this part in an exam essay rather than in coursework — check with your teacher)

8) **ORIGINAL WRITING** — Write <u>creative</u>, <u>imaginative</u> and <u>entertaining</u> stories about whatever takes your fancy really (although usually within some kind of guidelines). Sometimes you're asked to write in a certain style, e.g. for a newspaper.

The <u>Fun</u> Bit — Speaking and Listening

This part might not feel like an exam — but it's just as important to do well in it.

9) **SPEAKING AND LISTENING EXERCISE** — Communicate ideas by speaking. This could be tested through a <u>drama-based</u> activity, a <u>group</u> activity (e.g. a debate), an <u>individual presentation</u> or a combination of the three.

Let's talk about Exams baby, let's talk about you and me...

Yes OK, talking about Exams isn't the nicest way to start a book — but it's good to know exactly what's coming. It's going to get nicer, I promise. Go on, turn the page. Don't be scared. Go on...

Planning

You've got to make a plan for every single essay you ever write, whether it's for coursework or the exams. That's a plan on paper — not in your head. There are no shortcuts with planning.

Decide What to Say Before You Start

You've got to have a good think about what you're going to write about _before_ you start — otherwise your ideas won't follow a clear structure and you'll lose marks.

> _Good writing makes a point. It doesn't just ramble on about nothing._

Whatever kind of essay you're writing, make sure you've got _enough ideas_ to keep you writing till your time's up — without having to waffle. Waffle won't get you any marks at all.

Stick Your Points Down On Paper

1) Jot down a _plan_ of the points you want to make before you start writing.

2) That way you won't get to the end and realise you've _forgotten_ something.

3) Don't bother writing your plan in proper sentences — it's a waste of time.

4) In the exams spend _5 MINUTES_ planning every essay.

> Q. Write an article for a newspaper about an issue that's important to you. Explain why you think the issue is important.

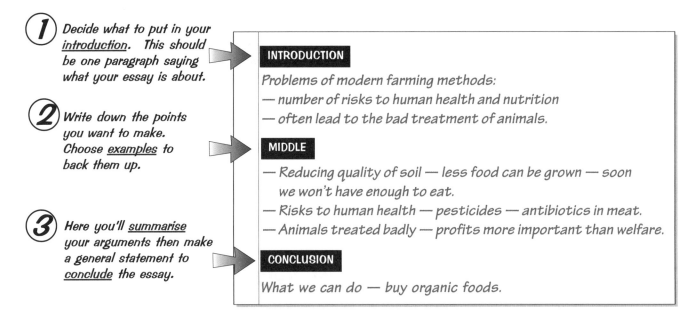

1 Decide what to put in your _introduction_. This should be one paragraph saying what your essay is about.

INTRODUCTION

Problems of modern farming methods:
— number of risks to human health and nutrition
— often lead to the bad treatment of animals.

2 Write down the points you want to make. Choose _examples_ to back them up.

MIDDLE

— Reducing quality of soil — less food can be grown — soon we won't have enough to eat.
— Risks to human health — pesticides — antibiotics in meat.
— Animals treated badly — profits more important than welfare.

3 Here you'll _summarise_ your arguments then make a general statement to _conclude_ the essay.

CONCLUSION

What we can do — buy organic foods.

Now you've done your plan you should be ready to start belting out your essay. Basically planning gets all the tricky thinking out the way as quickly as possible. Once you start writing you can make the best possible use of the time you've got.

No rambling — so no walking boots needed...

Writing that rambles on without getting anywhere isn't going to get you good marks. All this needs to be second nature by the time you get to the Exam, so get learning.

Starting Your Essay

You need to write a clear and punchy introduction to your essay — no waffle allowed. Waffling won't get you anywhere. Yes, definitely avoid waffling without saying anything. It's just waffle...

Start With a Good Introduction

In your introduction you've got to introduce the _overall point_ that your essay is making — and do it clearly.

> The introduction gives a _brief answer_ to the question.
> The rest of the essay _expands_ on your answer and gives _evidence_ for it.

Q. Why do you think Harper Lee chose Scout as the narrator in _To Kill A Mockingbird_?

It's fine to make a _personal statement_ in the introduction. Just don't keep using "I" all the way through the essay (see P. 6).

It makes it easier to answer the question if you use _similar wording_.

I believe that _Harper Lee chose Scout as the narrator in To Kill A Mockingbird_ because her youthful innocence provides a contrasting backdrop against which the story's themes of prejudice and hate can unfold.

You've said what you think and _clearly answered the question_. The rest of the essay can now back this up with examples from the text.

Grab the Reader's Attention at the Start

Use the introduction to grab the examiner's attention and make them want to read on. There are 3 different ways of doing this:

Q. Is testing beauty products on animals justified? Write an essay giving your opinion.

1) Use _strong, emotive language_ to get your opinion across, especially in persuasive essays.

Testing beauty products on animals is an _unforgivable_ and unjustifiable _evil_ in this so-called age of technology. It is a _bitter reminder_ of the human race's _obsession_ with vanity.

2) Say something _controversial_. You'll only lose marks if you can't back it up.

Use forceful language in your statement...

Testing beauty products on animals is _too often written off as being unjustified_. In the developed world, we expect a certain standard of living and, _without animal testing, our lives would be significantly less easy_.

...as long as you back it up.

3) Start with a _short, quirky statement_ for immediate impact.

Animals do not use beauty products. With this in mind, it seems unjustified that they should suffer for the continued development of such products.

Examiners have to mark tons of papers — if you can make yours stand out then they'll _want_ to give you marks for making their job less dull.

The intro is v. important — it's the only bit they actually read... (just kidding)

No, but the introduction is very important — it sets the scene for the whole essay. If you do a really good, attention-grabbing one, you'll put Mr Examiner in a good mood right from start. His name is Douglas by the way, if that helps.

Paragraphs

In the heat of the exam it's easy to forget to start new paragraphs, but you've got to use them properly if you want to get a C or above.

Paragraphs Make Your Writing Clearer

1) A <u>paragraph</u> is a group of sentences. These sentences are about the same thing, or follow on from each other.

2) All of the sentences in a paragraph are <u>related</u> to each other.

3) You need to start a new paragraph every time <u>something new</u> has happened.

...before he went home.

The street was quiet and very dark. Alex walked on tiptoes, trying to make as little noise as possible. He kept wondering what might be lurking around the next corner.

Suddenly Alex heard a faint noise. Could it be the dreaded peanut-butter monster?

The <u>ideas</u> in this paragraph are all about Alex walking down the street. When something new happens, you start a <u>new paragraph</u>.

Start a New Paragraph Every Time Something Changes

Each Time a New Person Speaks

Someone new is <u>speaking</u> so you need to change paragraph.

"I'll find him," muttered Donald. "He won't get away this time."

"What makes you so sure?" asked Mickey.

"What's going on guys?" A figure stepped out of the darkness. It was Elvis.

When You Start Writing About a Different Time

The first paragraph is about <u>five o'clock</u>.

This one's gone forward to a <u>different time</u>.

Here's one about the <u>past</u>.

By five o'clock, Edwin was angry. Shirley was late again, and the flower he'd bought was starting to droop.

Six o'clock came, and still she didn't appear. Enough was enough. Stuffing his flower into a rubbish bin, Edwin went home.

Three years before, Edwin had been stood up. He had never seen or heard from the girl again, and he didn't fancy going through another emotional crisis.

When You Start Writing About a New Place

This paragraph is about the playing fields.

Here's a new paragraph because this is happening <u>somewhere else</u>.

The playing fields were quiet and peaceful. There was no one around except Pete. He listened to the song of the distant birds and sighed happily.

Further down the valley, a huge cloud of dust rose into the summer sky, as the rebel elephant army raced towards the school. They were coming to free the students.

When You Talk About a New Person

This paragraph is about Liam.

Time for a new paragraph — there's a <u>new person</u>.

Liam sat on the side of the stage. He couldn't believe it. His guitar was broken, and without it he wouldn't be able to play at the school concert.

Then he saw Keith. Keith was a skinny, ill-looking boy who always got picked on. He was carrying an enormous guitar case.

Changing paragraphs — any time, any place...

Remember, start a new paragraph whenever you change the person speaking, the people, the place or the time. You've got to do it to keep old Douglas (the examiner) happy.

Paragraphs

Knowing when to use paragraphs will only get you so far.
To get an A*, A or B you've got to make your paragraphs flow on from each other.

Each Paragraph Needs a Clear Topic

Make only _one point_ in each paragraph. You'll lose marks if the examiner can't follow your argument.

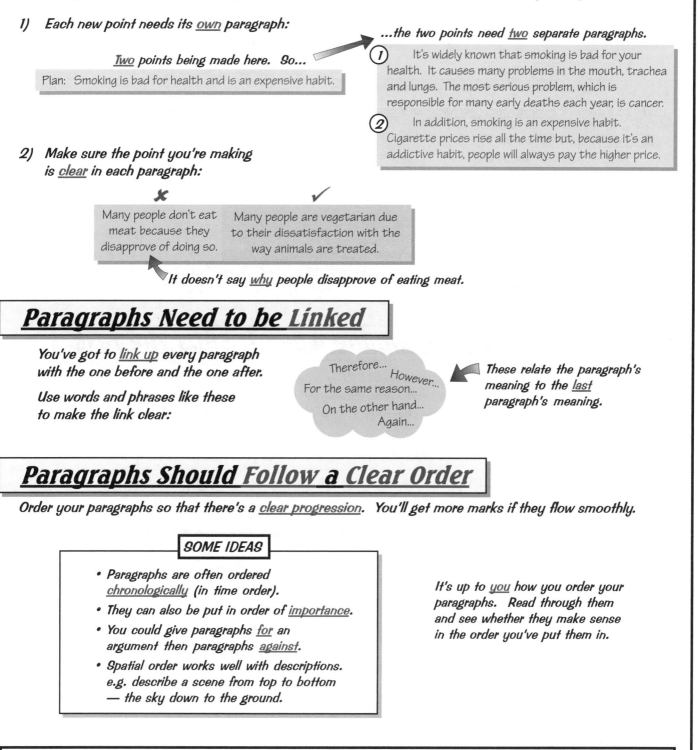

1) Each new point needs its _own_ paragraph:

Two points being made here. So...

Plan: Smoking is bad for health and is an expensive habit.

...the two points need _two_ separate paragraphs.

① It's widely known that smoking is bad for your health. It causes many problems in the mouth, trachea and lungs. The most serious problem, which is responsible for many early deaths each year, is cancer.

② In addition, smoking is an expensive habit. Cigarette prices rise all the time but, because it's an addictive habit, people will always pay the higher price.

2) Make sure the point you're making is _clear_ in each paragraph:

✗ Many people don't eat meat because they disapprove of doing so.

✓ Many people are vegetarian due to their dissatisfaction with the way animals are treated.

It doesn't say _why_ people disapprove of eating meat.

Paragraphs Need to be Linked

You've got to _link up_ every paragraph with the one before and the one after.

Use words and phrases like these to make the link clear:

Therefore...
However...
For the same reason...
On the other hand...
Again...

These relate the paragraph's meaning to the _last_ paragraph's meaning.

Paragraphs Should Follow a Clear Order

Order your paragraphs so that there's a _clear progression_. You'll get more marks if they flow smoothly.

SOME IDEAS

- Paragraphs are often ordered _chronologically_ (in time order).
- They can also be put in order of _importance_.
- You could give paragraphs _for_ an argument then paragraphs _against_.
- Spatial order works well with descriptions. e.g. describe a scene from top to bottom — the sky down to the ground.

It's up to _you_ how you order your paragraphs. Read through them and see whether they make sense in the order you've put them in.

Paragraphs — they do more than you think...

Paragraphs give structure to your essay and break it into separate points so it's easier for the examiner to read. Which is great. But I bet you didn't know you can also use them to send txt messages, voice mails and even to play music. Yep, paragraphs are the future, my friend...

Formal and Informal Language

In general essays, you'll get more marks if you write in formal language.
BUT you need to know when you should use informal language instead.

And then I want you to clean the cat, then take the cat into the garden and make it dirty, then clean it again. Then you can kill Malcolm for me.

Write **in** Formal Language

You need to use _formal language_ in your essays if you want to get anything above a D. Using formal language means doing certain things:

1) Be accurate and _concise_. Don't be chatty — that means no slang:

> I reckon Lady Macbeth wore the trousers in that household — she wasn't half bossy towards her old man. ✗

> Lady Macbeth was a forceful, manipulative character, who had a strong influence over her husband. ✓

2) Use correct _punctuation_, _grammar_ and _spelling_ (SEE SECTION 10).

3) _Don't say "I"_ this and "I" that — just talk about the question, the text, the characters, the style, etc.

> I think that the language in the poem evokes a melancholy mood. For example, I believe that the imagery of the white blossom turning brown symbolises the tainting of love by betrayal.

4) Don't use _clichés_:

YUK — nothing original is being said, so no marks here.

> The _atmosphere was electric_ in the court-room. The judge looked _as old as the hills_ in his white wig. It was _weird_ seeing my husband being sent down but, _at the end of the day_, there are _plenty more fish in the sea_.

5) Don't use _vague_ words like 'nice' or 'weird'.

Only Use Informal Language **When It** Suits The Task

1) Use formal language for all _general_ essays. BUT — sometimes you'll be asked to write in a certain style, e.g. for a tabloid newspaper. Here you're being tested on how well you _adapt_ your style to suit your audience — and formal language won't always be appropriate:

> Q. Write an article for a tabloid **OR** broadsheet newspaper about government plans to impose road tolls.

TABLOID

> The government has come up with yet another 'foolproof' plan to get cars off the roads — but it means that drivers had better start saving their pennies. People are fuming at the new plans to make drivers pay road tolls. Do they really think such an unpopular scheme will work?

Need to adapt the language by being less formal.

BROADSHEET

> Following lengthy discussions, the government has disclosed plans for a new solution to the problem of overcrowded roads in Britain: the construction of toll-roads. The proposals have proved unpopular with many road users, who doubt its potential for success.

Formal language is OK here.

2) In _original writing_ you're expected to write in a more creative way — i.e. NOT in formal language. You'll be marked on how well you create moods and feelings with your words.

The words create an eerie mood.

> The wind screamed through the trees, whipping branches into a frenzy and scattering leaves into the air in a manic, whirling dance.

> The gale-force wind caused branches to move considerably and leaves to fall to the ground.

Formal language just doesn't have the same mood-creating effect, somehow...

Could you inform Al that I wrote this page for Mal...

Uh oh, there's the first tumbleweed of the book...

So basically, you've got to use formal language in your essays unless the question _tells you_ to do otherwise. And if you want to be _really_ well prepared, watch plenty of Hugh Grant films too. I reckon this could be the year they ask you to write in the style of Hugh Grant. I just have a feeling...

Giving Evidence and Quoting

You've got to get this stuff right or you'll lose loads of marks in the exam and in coursework.
You have to give evidence for what you say and you have to quote your sources of evidence.

Give an Example Every Time You Make a Point

If you don't give examples for what you write, the examiners can't tell if you know what you're talking about.
They're not going to give you marks for something which could just be completely made up.

The woman was cruel to her dog.

This answer doesn't give any reasons...

...but this answer gives examples to justify the point it makes. That's loads better.

The woman was cruel to her dog. She kept him chained up in the sun all day, with very little food and no water.

Not giving examples to back up your points is the road to losing loads and loads of marks.

Use the 4 Picky Rules for Quoting

Quoting means using someone else's words to back up your arguments. Put quotation marks (" ") round quotes to separate other people's words from your words.

The quotation marks separate your words...

...from Mr. Wright's words.

Mr. Wright claimed that "there was no other possible course of action."

PICKY RULES

1) Use *exactly* the same words and punctuation as the person you're quoting used.

2) Always keep the same *meaning* — e.g. you couldn't quote "she approved of the idea" if the original was "she pretended that she approved of the idea."

3) Always say *where* you got the quote from. This means putting who said the quote and when they said it in brackets after it: "Vegetarians are healthier than meat-eaters" (The Vegetarian Society, 2002).

4) You don't need quotation marks if you *rephrase* someone else's words:

Mrs. Priya says, "Reading greatly improves vocabulary."

Direct quote

Mrs. Priya claims that a good way to improve vocabulary is through reading.

Rephrased words

Writing Must Flow Around Quotes

Insert your quotes so the words around them still make sense and flow well:

X *Doesn't make much sense*

A representative said, "Encouraging children to explore drama is our top priority." The board has agreed to finance the drama workshops.

✓ *Ideas flow much better*

The board has agreed to finance the drama workshops. A representative said, "Encouraging children to explore drama is our top priority."

Insert short quotes into your paragraphs (as in the example above). BUT — long quotes need their own paragraph. They don't need quotation marks but they do still need to be cited:

...blah blah blah blah blah blah blah:

Quote quote quote quote quote quote quote quote quote quote quote quote quote quote quote quote.
(Spencer 2001, 2)

Blah blah blah blah blah blah blah blah blah blah blah blah...

Leave a line above and below the quote.

"Quotes are great" (CGP, 2002)

You'll definitely improve your grade if you make sure you put loads of good examples and quotes in your answers. And you can — QUOTE — me on that. Ha ha... ... ...oh, I'm so funny.... .... hmmm.

Concluding and Checking

You've got to conclude your essay and check it over — but it shouldn't be a last-minute rushed job. You'll pick yourself up loads more marks by doing it thoroughly and carefully.

Bring Together the Key Points In Your Conclusion

Q. Write an essay explaining why backpacking is popular as a form of travel.

1) Start a new paragraph by going back to the *original question*.

2) Restate the *main points* of your essay briefly. This makes it clear how you've answered the question. Don't go on and on, though. Be focused.

> For many, there is no disputing the fact that backpacking is by far the best way to travel round different countries. It gives you the flexibilty and freedom to travel wherever you please, and it's great for meeting interesting fellow travellers along the way. It is also the cheapest form of travelling and allows those who would otherwise be unable to afford it to visit far-flung countries . It's good to know that, in a world where money and luxuries seem to rule, people still find the 'back to basics' lifestyle appealing.

3) Once you've summed up, write a final sentence to *conclude*.

Check Over Your Essay When You've Finished

1) Leave time at the end to *read through* your essay. Check that it makes sense, that you haven't got any facts wrong, and that it says what you want it to say.

| Macbeth |
| (Mcbath) |

2) Check the grammar, spelling and punctuation. If you find a mistake, put *brackets* round it, cross it out neatly with two lines through it and write the correction above.

3) If you've written something which isn't clear, put an *asterisk* * at the end of the sentence. Put another asterisk in the margin beside the sentence, and write what you mean in the margin.

| *He had him killed. | Macbeth wasn't nice to Banquo.* |

4) If you realise you should have started a new paragraph, put "//" to show where it starts.

Don't Panic If You Realise You've Gone Wrong

If you realise you've *forgotten* something obvious, write a note about it at the bottom of the final page, to tell the examiner. You'll get marks for noticing your mistake.

Never cross out your *whole essay* if you realise it's wrong. Don't panic, just continue the essay, explaining to the examiner why it's wrong. If there's time, tell them what the real answer is.

Don't give up if you're running out of time: even with only five minutes left, there's still time to pick up extra marks.

Check Coursework Extra Carefully

Examiners will be far more strict when marking *coursework essays* — because there's no excuse not to check your coursework essays really carefully. Read them over and over again until there are no mistakes. Use a dictionary to check spelling.

You can check-em any time you like, but you can never leave. (Guitar solo) ...

Oh wow, what a great page. It's one major tip-fest. I know you probably want to just read it again and again, but look up there ↗ at those beautiful questions waiting for you. Ooo, you jammy sausage.

Revision Summary

Every now and then throughout this book, you'll find pages like this one. They may look as dull as the National Lottery programme, but they're really important, so _DON'T SKIP THEM!_

You've read the section, but do you know it? Here's where you find out, right here, right now.

Do _all_ these questions without cheating, then go turn back and look up the bits you didn't know. Check them, and do the _whole lot again_ until you get 100% correct. GO.

1) Write down every type of essay you have to do for English GCSE.

2) What's the difference between an 'arguing' essay and an 'explaining' essay?

3) Explain what 'speaking and listening' exercises are.

4) Why is planning your essays a good idea?

5) Should your plan be written in proper sentences? Why?

6) How long (roughly) should you spend planning an essay?

7) Should your essay-writing style be a) precise, b) full of waffle or c) full of waffles?

8) Complete this sentence — "A good plan needs an introduction, a middle bit and a ....".

9) What should a good introduction do?

10) Should the question you're answering play a part in your introduction?

11) Why should you try to grab the reader's attention right at the start of your essay?

12) When saying something controversial, should you a) write in capital letters, b) always have evidence to back it up or c) stand on the desk and yell "shove it" at your fellow students?

13) Why should you write your essays using paragraphs?

14) Which of these would be a reason to start a new paragraph — a) when a new person speaks, b) when you write about a new place or a new time and c) when you're hungry?

15) Say why your ideas need to flow clearly from paragraph to paragraph.

16) Write a definition of what 'formal' writing is.

17) Rewrite the following sentence so that it is formal and grammatically correct — "theres no way lady macbeth was a really nice woman cos she was well bossy with her fella"

18) "Duncan was as _dead as the dodo_" — what's wrong with this sentence and why?

19) Explain why there is no single writing style you can practise for your 'original writing' essays.

20) Why do you need to give evidence for the points you make in your essays?

21) Why do you need to say where you got your quotes from?

22) Do you need to use quotation marks when you paraphrase someone else's words?

23) What should a good conclusion do for your reader?

24) Explain why it's a good idea to leave yourself time at the end of the exam to check through your essay.

25) What's the best thing to do if you realise that the essay you've written (in an exam) has failed to answer the question?

26) Explain why you need to spend more time checking and polishing your coursework essays than your exam essays.

Answering Literature Questions

It's not just writing a <u>book review</u>, you know. There are different <u>types</u> of literature questions and <u>you</u> need to know how to answer <u>all</u> of them. Come on, it's only a few pages — how bad can it be...

Step 1 — Work Out What The Questions Are About

1) You have to <u>answer the question properly</u> to get a decent grade.

2) The first thing to do is work out what the question is about.

3) The two subjects that come up time and again are the <u>writer's message</u> and the <u>characters</u>:

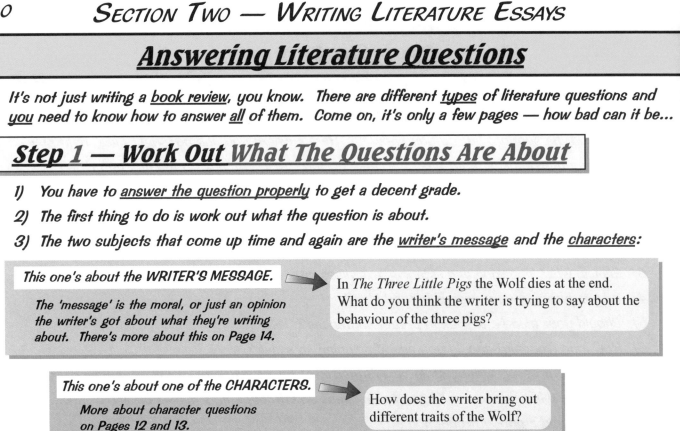

This one's about the **WRITER'S MESSAGE.**

The 'message' is the moral, or just an opinion the writer's got about what they're writing about. There's more about this on Page 14.

In *The Three Little Pigs* the Wolf dies at the end. What do you think the writer is trying to say about the behaviour of the three pigs?

This one's about one of the **CHARACTERS.**

More about character questions on Pages 12 and 13.

How does the writer bring out different traits of the Wolf?

4) For the 'different cultures and traditions' question in the English exam, you'll also have to write about the writer's <u>background</u>, and how it links with the poem or story. *(See P.15)*

Compare *The Enormous Turnip* with *The Enormous Beetroot* showing how the writers reveal their ideas and feelings about the cultures in which they have set their stories.

5) Once you know what the questions are about, you're ready to <u>choose</u> between them.

Step 2 — Choose the Question That's Best For You

1) You always get a <u>choice</u> with literature questions.

2) There's usually a choice of two questions on each book.

3) For questions on stuff from the Anthology you could get a choice of three questions.

4) <u>Obviously</u> you want to choose a question that you can answer really well, but in the hot sweaty panic of the first few minutes of the exam, it's easy to make a duff choice.

5) Don't panic. Take a deep breath, and then choose:

- A question which gives you lots of **IDEAS** on what to write about.
- A question which is on material you're **FAMILIAR** with. (i.e. you've read the book, the poems or the stories)
- A question which you definitely **UNDERSTAND.**

6) If you're doing <u>coursework</u> this isn't such a big deal. Just make sure you understand the question before you stay up all night writing your essay.

Choose wisely you must...

Hmmm... choices... Look, just PICK THE EASIEST ONE. Loads of people go wrong by picking the <u>most interesting</u> one, then find out it's <u>rock hard</u> once they start writing. <u>Don't</u> fall into that <u>trap</u>.

Answering Literature Questions

Where to start... where to start...
Got writer's block? Fear not — the CGP Guide to Starting Your Essay will set you on your way.

Step 3 — Break The Question Into Bullet Points

1) You *can't* just give a one-sentence answer to literature questions.

Does Little Red Riding Hood change at all in the course of the story?
Write about **two** episodes, one at the beginning of the story and one at the end, showing how she changes or stays the same.

2) You have to *go into detail* and make lots of *separate points*.

3) If you're doing *Foundation* the exam paper helps you by breaking the question down into bullets:

Write about:
• what she says and does
• her attitudes and feelings
• how the writer shows you how she changes or stays the same.

Figure out the first
2 things and it'll help
you work out the answer.

4) If you're doing *Higher* you'll have to break the question into bullets yourself.
Ask your teacher for a stack of old literature Foundation papers so you can practise.

5) Scribble a plan based on the bullet points.

• BEGINNING - picking flowers, no hurry to get to Grandma's; END - she tricks wolf
• BEGINNING - feels confident and secure; END - cross with herself, more confident
• BEGINNING - "drifted along", compares her to butterfly; END - looks the wolf in the eye, "now she knew what to do"

Choose things that can be compared to show how she changes.

Step 4 — Write A General Answer Then Follow the Plan

You can make your introduction *pretty short* — just make sure it gives a quick answer
to the question so the examiner has a rough idea of what you're going to say.

There are several episodes in the story which show how Little Red Riding Hood changes —
in particular the flower-picking in the forest glade, and the escape from Grandmother's house.
They show how Little Red Riding Hood starts off naive, but learns from her experience.

The rest of your essay should *back up* what you say in the introduction.

1) Keep your essay clear by dealing with the bullet points in order.
2) Don't chop and change between different ideas. Deal with
one at a time and use a separate paragraph for each one.

Step 5 — Don't Forget The Conclusion

Run through all your points *briefly* in your conclusion and sum up.
Make sure your summing-up answers the original question.

At the start of the story Little Red Riding Hood doesn't have a care in the world.
By the end she has been through a terrifying experience. The writer shows that
she has learnt from her experience and become more wary and cautious.

Break the question up — before it breaks you down...

If there's not enough in your plan, there won't be enough in your essay. Simple as that.
Get the planning right and not only will the essay be easier to write, it'll be a better essay.

Writing About Characters

This character stuff seems obvious — but it's not. So there. And I'm jolly well going to write a whole page telling you how to pick out the non-obvious stuff about characters. And you're going to read it.

Find Bits Where The Writer Describes the Characters

1) The writer will <u>deliberately</u> describe characters in a way that tells you what he or she wants you to think about them.

2) Find descriptions of how they look or act.

> **BASE DETAILS — SIEGFRIED SASSOON**
> The majors are described as "scarlet" and "fierce, bald, and short of breath". It makes them sound like grumpy old men, not soldiers.

Find Evidence For What They're Like In What They Do

It's the same whether you're writing about a book, a play, or a poem — look at what people do, then write down <u>what that says about them</u>.

> **OF MICE AND MEN — JOHN STEINBECK**
> Lennie can't help hurting the puppies when he strokes them — he isn't in control of his own strength.

> **KING LEAR — SHAKESPEARE**
> There can be no doubt about Regan and Goneril's cruelty, after they turned against their father in Act 2.

Work Out The Reasons Why Characters Do Things

When you're writing about what a character does, always say <u>why</u> they do it.

1) Some characters are motivated by stuff like...

2) Some characters want things so badly it leads them to <u>manipulate</u> others.

> Pity   Fear   Love   Money
> Anger   Greed   Food
> Power   (well sometimes)

3) Some characters want to be <u>liked</u>.

4) Some characters do things for <u>revenge</u> or to prove they have <u>power</u> over another character.

Look At The Way Characters Speak

1) The way characters, including the narrator, <u>speak</u> tells you a lot about them.

2) This is true for poetry, plays and prose.

> "Oh, you're one of those little men who reads the gas meters? How hilarious..."

stuck up and rude

> "So, erm, do you think it would be alright, I mean if you didn't mind, could you possibly... pass the salt please, Dad?"

painfully shy

How did Ewan McGregor break his leg?...

Evidence is <u>no good whatsoever</u> if you don't use it. Describe your character in <u>as much detail</u> as you can. Use <u>all</u> your bits of evidence — and <u>plenty of quotes</u> to back up everything you say.

Writing About Characters

_This stuff should be going through your head whenever you've got a Characters question.
You can't fail to pick up marks if you talk about these things..._

Look At How The Characters Treat Other People

_You can tell a lot about the main characters by watching how they get on with others.
It can reveal sides to their character that they keep hidden from the other main characters._

> Everyone loved Jack. His family, his friends, and everyone who knew him thought he was warm and caring.
> Jack was getting into a cab, when a homeless man shuffled up and asked him for change. Jack spat into the man's face, saying "Don't ever speak to me again old man, or you'll be sorry."

Although people believe Jack is warm and caring, in reality he is rude and mean.

Stories Tell You What Characters Think

1) _Novels and short stories give descriptions of characters' thoughts and behaviour —
   the voice telling the story fills you in on what characters are thinking._

2) _Pinpoint those bits, quote them, and say how they help answer the question._

> Sarah was disgusted by Jamie's behaviour at the bar and refused to speak to him.

Sarah has a very low opinion of the way Jamie behaves at the bar, which suggests that at this point in the book, she still hasn't forgiven him for causing the car crash.

3) _Books with a third person narrator (who isn't one of the characters),
   let you in on the secret thoughts of all the characters._

> Tamasine didn't want to tell anyone that she was ill. Of all her friends, no one suspected except Caitlin, and Caitlin didn't feel comfortable talking to anyone about it. If Caitlin had known how upset Tamasine was, she would have helped.

The narrator = the person telling the story.

First Person Narrators Can't Always Be Trusted

1) _Books that are written in the first person — so the story's told by one of the
   characters — give you a picture of that character all the way through. You get
   a first hand description of exactly what the character sees, says, and thinks._

2) _Find bits where they tell you what they're like,
   or give away what they're like by their attitudes._

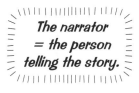

> I've never been a nice person.

3) _Don't take what they say for granted though —
   you're only getting one side of the story._

> That evening I went to a dinner party. If there's one thing I can't stand it's a group of people enjoying themselves. It makes me sick.

> All the other people there were so boring. No one had anything interesting to say to me, and there wasn't a single one there that wasn't a fool.

The narrator feels that he is superior to the other guests, even though they all find him dull.

...He slipped out of character...

You don't need to write about all this stuff for every Character essay. Just have a look and see if any of it's there in the text. If it's there, you can use it to grab a great armful of marks...

The Writer's Message

<u>All</u> authors have an <u>axe to grind</u>. All <u>you</u> need to do is spot what <u>kind of axe</u> it is... *or something.*
Anyway, this page is all about how to <u>spot the author's message</u> (axe) and how to <u>write about it</u>.

Message Questions Can Be Hard To Spot

1) Questions about the message can be worded in all sorts of different ways:

> When the Woodcutter kills the Wolf what is the writer trying to show?

> Why do you think the Woodcutter is important?

> What does *The Three Little Pigs* have to say about architecture?

2) They're all asking the <u>same</u> thing:

> *What does the writer think? Write about all the bits of the text that give it away.*

3) Work out what the message of the text is, and then
    write about all the bits which helped you work it out.

Work Out the Message of Your Set Texts Before the Exams

Obviously if you work out the message of your set texts <u>before</u> the exams you'll have a lot less to
worry about on the day. If you haven't read the texts yet, this is a great way to get a quick <u>overview</u>:

This is what you could do for <u>The Grapes of Wrath</u> by John Steinbeck.

story
The Joad family lose their Oklahoma farm to a big corporation. They travel to California to find work as fruit pickers. The journey is tough, and life gets even tougher when they reach California.

characters
Characters who stick with the family do OK. Anyone who goes off on their own has a tough time. Characters in powerful positions like police and landowners are described in a negative way.

tone
Life back in Oklahoma is remembered with affection. In the camps in California, life is mostly sad and difficult.

title
"The grapes of <u>wrath</u>" is a big hint that Steinbeck is angry about the events he describes in his book.

Once you've looked at all that, put it all together to work out what the message is.
I'd say it's something like...

> The Great Depression had a terrible effect on the lives of ordinary people.

...or > It's important for people to help each other, however tough life gets.

The notes you've made about the story, the character, the tone and the title
are the <u>evidence</u> you need to back up the points you make in your essay.

The writer's message — your dinner's in the oven...

<u>Bold claims</u> need <u>backing up</u>. Otherwise you're just <u>ranting</u>. I've said it before and I'll say it
again — you need to <u>get evidence</u> from the text and <u>quote it</u> in your answer. OK, so it means
you have to <u>read the book properly</u>, but I guess that's just something you have to <u>live with</u>.

Different Cultures & Traditions

"Different Cultures" questions really <u>aren't that different</u> from any other ones. There's just a <u>few extra bits</u> to look out for. As if you didn't already have enough to think about...

There Are Two Big Things to Write About

There are <u>two</u> main types of "Different Cultures and Traditions" question:

> <u>How</u> the poems or stories are written

> Write about the same stuff as you would in any literature essay, but look out for these things too:
> 1) Unfamiliar words from other languages or dialects.
> 2) Words spelt so they sound like an accent or dialect.
> 3) The <u>form</u> of poems. It's a lot more varied in the "Different Cultures" poems than in the other ones you have to study.

> The main <u>thoughts and feelings</u>

> 1) Feelings about <u>differences between cultures</u> comes up all the time. It could be someone who's moved to a different country feeling out of place, or the contrast between rich and poor in one country.
> 2) A lot of the material for "Different Cultures and Traditions" is more <u>political</u> than anything you'll study by British writers. Look for views on equality and democracy.

Even if the question seems to ask <u>mainly</u> about the way things are written, DON'T ignore the thoughts and feelings. The same goes for questions about the thoughts and feelings — DON'T ignore the way the it's all written. If you totally ignore one thing, and don't write about the other you <u>won't get</u> a C or above.

The Examiners Just Want A Bit of Understanding

For the thoughts and feelings bit you have to show '<u>empathy</u>' with the writers' ideas and feelings. That doesn't mean you have to <u>agree</u> with what they say — it just means you have to <u>show you understand</u> the writers' points of view.

You also have to 'explore' the ideas in the work for a higher mark. That means <u>go into detail</u> and <u>be specific</u>.

So don't just say: | She is unhappy because she misses speaking her own language.

Say: | English is not the poet's mother tongue. Speaking English all the time makes her feel as though she is physically damaged. | **Much better** — shows you understand <u>why</u> she's unhappy, and exactly how she feels.

It Pays To Know About the Writers

The best <u>revision</u> you can do is read the Anthology. After that find out a bit about each of the writers, and note down how that links with their work. Don't <u>just</u> make notes. *LEARN THEM.*

1) Where the writer's from.
2) Where the writer lives now.
3) How the poem or story fits in with the writer's life story.

> GRACE NICHOLS, <u>Island Man</u>
> 1) Born in Guyana (Caribbean).
> 2) Has lived in the UK since 1977.
> 3) Sympathises with others living far from what is familiar.

You don't have to go on and on about this stuff in your essay. Just make sure you know it — it'll help you come up with ideas about what to say, and avoid saying anything <u>Embarrassingly Wrong</u>.

Back in my grandmother's village all the men wore petticoats...

For <u>Pete</u>'s sake — READ the Anthology. You usually have to <u>compare</u> (P. 18) so if you haven't read them, you're <u>scuppered</u>. But if you really <u>know your stuff</u> you could go up a <u>whole grade</u>.

The Writer's Techniques

Now you'd think that a page on style would be interesting, wouldn't you... Still, never mind, eh.
"You have to show that you understand the writer's style... blah de blah..." look, just get on with it.

Writing Style Affects The Way You Feel

The style of a text is a combination of features like these:

words you hear every day	short, simple sentences	lots of fancy comparisons	lots of action
unusual, difficult words	long, complicated sentences	no fancy comparisons	lots of description

The style influences the way you feel about characters, ideas and events.
Show the examiners you understand how the writer manages to affect the way you feel.

If you're saying a character is on the verge of insanity, show how the style backs it up.

The writer makes the character speak in a very confused way. ➡ MAC: I'm late - late - late, better late than never Mother said to me. I'm never late - never been better. So late, so late...

If you're saying you think the writer is disgusted by greed, show how the style backs it up.

The writer shows how he or she feels through a descriptive bit. ➡ All around me the round red faces of the customers shone with sweat and wine. A woman sitting alone in the corner raised a dripping slice of steak to her lips. Cream and blood ran down her chin and she laughed as the little terrier sitting in her lap licked it away.

Pay Attention to Settings

Writers just love using settings to mess with the way you feel about what's happening.

The candlelight cast huge shifting shadows on the mossy walls. The wind howled down the chimney, throwing sparks around the room.

"Dinner is served," the butler announced. The Count took my arm and led me to the dining room.

Creepy — could be human fluids for dinner.

The candlelight cast soft shadows around the room. I stretched out lazily in the armchair by the fire.

"Dinner is served," the butler announced. The Count took my arm and led me to the dining room.

Ah — that sounds a bit more enjoyable.

Look At The Order of Events

1) *Stories aren't always told in order.*
   Writers mess around with the order to keep you interested.

2) *Flashbacks are a favourite trick. What happens is that the story's going along nicely in the present, and suddenly the scene shifts to the week before, or some years before.*

3) *Foreshadowing gives clues about what will happen later on in the story.*

   At the start of Macbeth the Witches predict what will happen to Macbeth. ➡ *Everything they predict comes true — though not always in the way Macbeth expects.*

Rubber gloves — now they change how you feel...

You see — I reckon you just enjoy a book or you don't. I don't get why you have to do all this analysing. I mean what's the point. And why do we have to do English anyway. Hmmph.

Useful Literature Words

Argghhh... the curse of English... horrible literature terms... NOOOooo......
OK — deep breath. Don't panic. Whatever you do, don't panic... I SAID DON'T PANIC!!!

Use These Words — __AND GET THEM RIGHT__

There's a lot to learn here — but these words are really useful.
Don't just learn how to spell them. Learn what they really mean.

simile | A simile compares one thing to another. Similes often use the words 'like' and 'as'.

Don't get these two mixed up.

> His socks stank like a dead dog.

> His dog was as mean as an old bandito.

metaphor | Metaphors describe one thing as if it were another. Metaphors never use 'like' or 'as'.

> My car is a heap of old rubbish.

> But soft — what light through yonder window breaks. It is the East, and Juliet is the Sun.

imagery | If you're not sure whether you're writing about a metaphor or a simile then just call it 'imagery' — it's the general term for comparisons like metaphors and similes.

symbolism | Making an object stand for an emotion or idea.

> Harry's pigeons flew high above the dismal suburban gardens.

> If Harry wanted to leave home, the pigeons could be a symbol of freedom.

allegory | A story where characters and settings can stand for something else.

The Crucible by Arthur Miller describes a witch-hunt in a small town in 17th-century America.

Really it's about a period in the 1950s when the US government started accusing artists and film-makers of being Communists.

ambiguity | Words or events have more than one possible meaning. If you notice something that could be interpreted in two or three different ways then say so — that's A and A* material.

irony | The words say one thing, but the writer means something else. Say Carter is awful at football, and has played badly in a game. The author writes:

> Carter really excelled himself this time.

He's being ironic — he actually means "Carter played even worse than usual."

> **WARNING** — if you use these words and get them wrong you'll end up looking a bit pretentious, and a bit stupid. If you can see a writer's used some clever technique but you're not sure what to call it, then just describe it in your own words.

My sister never strokes cats — she's got an allegory...

Arthur Miller was a weedy-looking bloke, but he was married to Marilyn Monroe. It just shows. Using those tricky words will get you marks. They're difficult, but they're very, very useful.

Comparing

"This poem's better than that one" won't get you anywhere. Trust me, I tried it once.
One last page on Literature Essays and it'll all be over. And this one's a beaut, I can assure you.

Comparing = Finding Similarities And Differences

You have to look at two or more things *together*.

Compare these two poems. You should consider:
– the language used
– the ideas they contain
– how the poem is presented

This example is about two poems, but you could be asked to compare any of your texts — including media texts...

You've got to describe the *similarities* and *differences* between the poems for *each* of these points.

Compare Both Things in Every Paragraph

The whole point of these questions is that you write about both things *together*. It's about *MAKING LINKS* between them. If you tackle each point in the question in turn, it's like having your own ready-made essay plan.

1 – the language used

You need to say whether the language is *similar* or *different* in the two poems, along with examples to prove your point.

The language used in 'The Laboratory' is very simple, almost as if the narrator were in a hurry to tell his story without paying attention to his wording. The language used in 'Ulysses' is far more complex and doesn't rhyme.

2 – the ideas they contain

Here you need to look at the ideas in both poems. You're trying to *make links* between ideas that are *similar* and ideas that are *different*.

Ulysses is a noble but weary warrior — he seems proud when he says he has "drunk delight of battle with my peers". In contrast, the main character in 'The Laboratory' is bitter towards the woman he is trying to poison — he says "He is with her... they laugh, laugh at me".

3 – how the poem is presented

You have to write about the *structure* of the two poems for this bit of the question — say why they are *similar* or *different*.

'The Laboratory' features very short sentences and verses, which has the effect of conveying the excitement of the narrator. The verses in 'Ulysses' are much longer, which makes the poem feel less frantic.

You could be asked to compare other things too...

imagery   message   setting   structure   characters

...so if you think about these things *before* the exam, you'll be sorted.

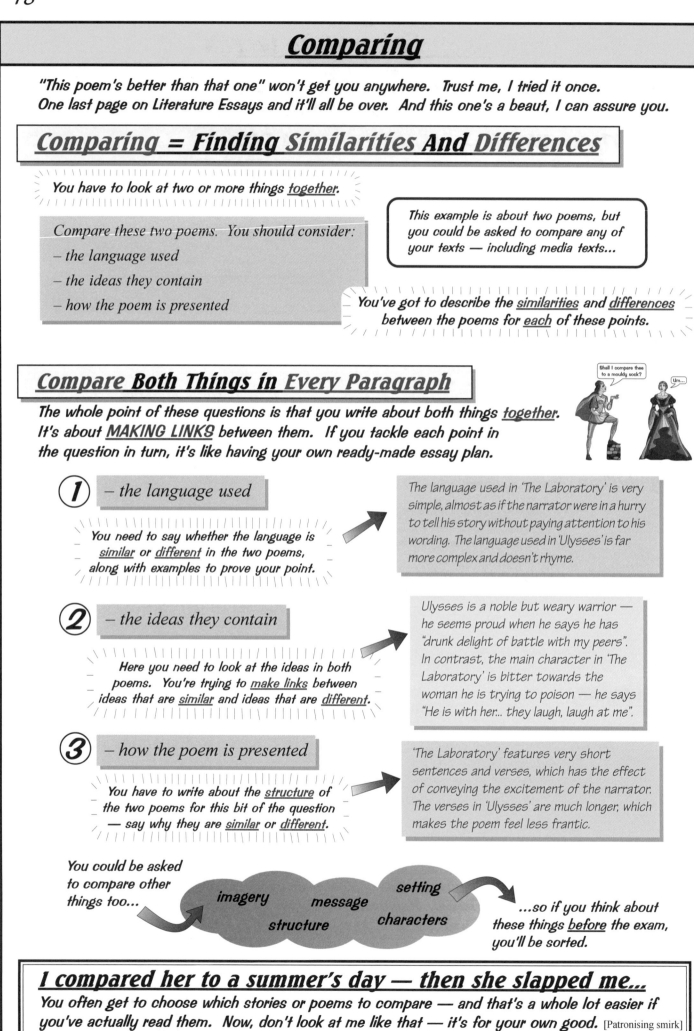

I compared her to a summer's day — then she slapped me...

You often get to choose which stories or poems to compare — and that's a whole lot easier if you've actually read them. Now, don't look at me like that — it's for your own good. [Patronising smirk]

Revision Summary

There's _literally_ (ho ho) just one page left till this section is over. Keep going — these questions are a darned good measure of what you've taken in and what's dribbled out of your earholes.

You know what kind of questions are gonna come up. And you know the five-step guide to writing your answer will make it all a whole lot easier. True, there are all those annoying technical bits to learn — but just think how good it'll feel to know exactly what you're on about in that exam...

1) What two subjects are most likely to come up in your literature exam questions?

2) What's the extra topic you'll have to write about for the 'different cultures and traditions' question?

3) Write down the five steps you should follow to answer an essay question well. Give a short explanation of each step.

4) What should you put in a good conclusion?

5) Explain four things you could talk about when you're writing about characters.

6) What is a third person narrator?

7) What is first person narrator? Why can't you take what they say for granted?

8) Message questions can be hard to spot — but what is the one thing that they'll all essentially be asking you?

9) Give four areas you could look at if you were working out the message of a set text before an exam.

10) You're writing about different cultures and traditions. What are the two big things you would talk about? Write a quick paragraph explaining each one.

11) What is empathy?
    a) Showing you understand the writer's point of view
    b) Talking about your own point of view
    c) Showing you don't know what you're talking about

12) What do you need to do to explore the ideas in a work properly?

13) What would it pay to know about each of the authors in the anthology?

14) List any four features of writing style.

15) Explain how the style of a text can influence the person reading it.

16) Explain what authors use settings for.

17) What are flashbacks?
    a) The parts where the scene shifts to an earlier time
    b) The bits that don't make any sense
    c) The things they use to put streaks in your hair

18) What is foreshadowing?

19) Write a short explanation of what each of these technical words means:
    i) simile   ii) metaphor   iii) imagery   iv) symbolism
    v) allegory   vi) ambiguity   vii) irony

20) Explain what you have to do when comparing two texts.

21) What should you make sure you do in every paragraph of a comparison essay?

22) You're preparing for the exam. List five things you could compare in texts beforehand.

What The Examiner Wants

Basically, the examiner wants to know that you've understood the play. It's as simple as that.
And if you bung in a few quotes from appropriate places, you're already halfway there.

Show You've Understood the Play

1) The examiner wants to know you understand _the order_ everything happens in. This is quite
   simple — you just have to avoid making stupid mistakes like "Juliet kills herself in Act 1".

2) The examiner wants to know you're familiar with _all_ the characters, not just the main
   ones. So, it'll look really good if you refer to some minor characters in your answer.

   > You've also got to know stuff _about_ the characters — who's related to whom, what
   > are they like, how they behave, etc... If you get people mixed up, you'll lose marks.

3) You need to _quote_ little bits of text every now and then,
   to back up your points and prove you've understood the play.

Explain the Major Issues the Play Deals With

Plays are about more than just the plot — they deal with wider issues.
Look out for these 3 things in any play — you'll boost your grade if you mention them:

1 Social Issues   'Death of a Salesman' deals with the American Dream of the self-made man.

2 Moral Issues   'An Inspector Calls' deals with what drives people to suicide.

3 Philosophical Issues   Lots of Shakespeare's plays ask questions about what love
actually is, not just how people act when they're in it.

Show You Know that Plays Should be Watched not Read

You need to show that you realise plays are meant to be _performed_, not read silently.

The examiner wants to know you've thought about the _impact_ a play would have on an audience.

You can do this easily by throwing in the odd line a bit like this —

> This would look particularly spectacular
> when performed on stage because of the...

> This is a visual joke that an audience
> would find very amusing because...

Come Up With Some Ideas of Your Own

1) Examiners _love it_ if you can come up with something _original_.

2) If something occurs to you but you're not sure if it's right, try and _stick it in_ anyway.

3) As long as you can back it up with a _QUOTE_ from the text, you're sorted.

Stop playing around — and get this learnt...

Remember that plays are meant to be acted, not read in your head. So if you're struggling, put
on your best thespian's voice and read it aloud — that way the characters will be clearer.

What The Examiner Wants

You always have to write about this stuff in drama essays — whether it's in exams or coursework. And hey whoop-dee-da — it all applies to Shakespeare plays too...

Write About the Style

1) The person marking wants you to go into <u>detail</u> about the language.

2) Say <u>which</u> effects you think they're trying to create. e.g. suspense, humour, anger, etc...

3) Mention any <u>imagery</u> — there's plenty in drama.

    e.g. Playwrights use a lot of <u>personification</u>.

    This is when an object, or something in nature, is given human characteristics. It can bring the landscape to life, and make the mood more intense.

4) Mention any <u>repetition</u> — anything repeated is important.

> Go back to P. 17 and remind yourself what to look out for.

> ...Shall I believe
> That unsubstantial Death is amorous,
> And that the lean abhorred monster keeps
> Thee here in dark to be his paramour?
>
> Romeo and Juliet Act 5 Scene 3

Show You Understand the Significance of the Play

Almost all plays have something to say about <u>society</u> at the time they were written in — even lighthearted comedies and histories that were set in different periods.

WAR — What's the point? Is it a good thing?

JUSTICE — What makes a good ruler? Can a ruler be just?

ORDER — Can we maintain order? Is chaos inevitable?

LOVE — What is love? Is it always a good thing?

FATE — Do we control our own lives?

You need to think very carefully about which of these <u>themes</u> comes up, and what the playwright might have been trying to say.

Show You Appreciate Stagecraft

'Stagecraft' means the writer's skill at writing for the stage. Appreciating it means asking yourself a few key questions —

1 How would this scene look on stage?   **2** How would the audience react?   **3** Is it effective?

The final act of Romeo and Juliet features above average 'stagecraft':

> Romeo fights Paris in the tomb while the audience, knowing that Friar Lawrence is on his way, hope he'll arrive and avert this tragedy. But, he arrives too late. These events happen in a very short space of time and the tension is incredible. Even though we know from the start of the play that they'll both die, we still hope that they won't.

Stagecraft? — but I don't have a broomstick...

This is all worth learning for sure, as it's relevant for any play you end up studying. So learn the headings and mention them in any drama essay. Even ones about Shakespeare.

Reading Plays

You need to know how plays are <u>different</u> from books and poems to write about them properly. You can lose a whole barrel of marks if you ignore the fact that the text is a play.

Plays Can Be <u>Serious</u> or <u>Funny</u>

Tragedy

1) Tragedy is the most <u>serious</u> kind of play and is about <u>big topics</u> — e.g. religion, love, death, war.

2) Tragedies are meant to be really moving and often have a moral message.

3) Older tragedies are set in an <u>imaginary</u> or <u>past</u> world. The characters are often kings and queens or even gods and goddesses.

Comedy

1) Comedies are supposed to make you laugh.

2) Events and characters are based on things that happen <u>in real life</u>, but are much more silly and exaggerated.

Don't forget History Plays

They're any kind of play based on real historical events — dead popular with Shakespeare.

Dialogue <u>is</u> One Character Talking to Another

Write about dialogue to show how characters react. It looks like this on the page...

LORD CRUMB:	*Where exactly is the pizza?*
VERNON:	*In the basement, my lord.*
LORD CRUMB:	*Very good, Vernon.*

If two or more people talk to each other it's called <u>dialogue</u>.
If one person speaks for a long time it's called a <u>monologue</u>.
If one character stage-whispers to the audience, but other characters <u>can't hear</u>, it's called an <u>aside</u>.

VERNON: (aside) *Well, it's not there yet, but it will be in 10 minutes.*

It's easy to spot because it says "<u>aside</u>" after the character's name.

*I wanted to be a cream puff, *sniff**

A Soliloquy is Thinking <u>Out Loud</u>

A soliloquy only involves <u>one character</u> (like a monologue). The character doesn't talk <u>to</u> anyone — they're just thinking out loud. <u>Only the audience</u> can hear what they're saying — other characters <u>can't hear a thing</u>.

Stage Directions <u>Give More Detail About the Story</u>

You can write about <u>stage directions</u> — they tell you a lot about how the playwright wanted the play to look.

STAGE DESIGNS
scenery, lighting, special effects

A cluttered attic room: stuffed bear, upright piano, pot plants. Moonlight filters through a dirty window.

The room is dirty and cluttered, so it sounds as if it's not well looked after.

ACTION

Unseen by Lord Crumb, Vernon slides the pizza into an envelope and conceals it beneath a cushion on the couch.

DIALOGUE
little details about how the actors say their lines

LORD CRUMB:		*I was wondering...*
VERNON:	(interrupts)	RUN!!!

I used to know a drama queen — but my parents disapproved...

If you ask me, soliloquy is a ridiculous sort of a word. It's not easy to spell, it looks odd, and yet all it means is talking to yourself. Who'd want to do a thing like that, eh?

Language in Shakespeare Texts

Shakespeare's language can seem a bit daunting — but don't be afraid, my little balls of fluff.
Examiners are impressed if you use the right words, so even a little goes a long way.

Show You're Aware of How Old (and Weird) It All Is

1) Shakespeare's plays are about <u>400 years old</u>,
   so it's not surprising the language is a bit strange.

2) The sense of <u>humour</u> was different too — lots of
   the jokes are <u>puns</u> (words with double meanings).

3) They also thought the idea of <u>girls dressing up as boys</u> was funny
   (basically because all the actors in Shakespeare's time were men,
   so boys dressed as women dressed as boys — get it?).

4) Mention the different sense of humour to show that you're aware of when the play was written.

Be Specific When You Write About Language

Shakespeare wrote in a mixture of poetry and prose. You can write about whether people are
posh or common, and are serious or joking around — just by looking at the <u>form</u> they speak in.

Poetic Verse is the Most Dramatic — and It Rhymes

1) Poetic verse is definitely the most
   dramatic one of the lot.

2) You can spot it easily because it has 10 or 11
   syllables in each line and it <u>rhymes</u>.

3) It sounds more impressive than the rest of the text,
   and is used especially by the posh characters and
   at the beginnings and ends of scenes.

> *From forth the fatal loins of these two foes*
> *A pair of star-cross'd lovers take their life,*
> *Whose misadventur'd piteous overthrows*
> *Doth with their death bury their parents' rage.*
>
> *Romeo and Juliet* The Prologue

Blank Verse Doesn't Rhyme

1) This is just like poetic verse, only harder to spot because it <u>doesn't rhyme</u> (but still has 10 or 11 syllables).
2) It sounds grander than plain old prose, but any of the characters can speak in it.
3) The majority of the lines are written in it.

> *If music be the food of love, play on;*
> *Twelfth Night*

> *Wilt thou be gone? It is not yet near day.*
> *Romeo and Juliet*

> *Badger V*
> *The badger laughs when'er he lets one rip.*

Prose Can Be Spoken By Anyone

The rest is written in normal prose, like this
paragraph. Prose is mainly for minor
characters, although anyone can talk in prose.

It's for general chatting, larking about or bits
that just move the plot along, and aren't
particularly meaningful.

> *FESTE: Vent my folly! I am afraid this great lubber,*
> *the world, will prove a cockney. I prithee*
> *now, ungird thy strangeness and tell me what*
> *I shall vent to my lady.*
>
> *Twelfth Night* Act 4 Scene 1

Language — no phonecall would ever be the same without it...

If you can just get all these terms out quickly and efficiently (and in the right places, obviously)
— the examiner will know you've got it sussed. And he'll give you a big ol' mark to show it.

What The Examiner Wants

Some questions are phrased in a difficult way, but actually loads of them are quite similar.
If you know what you're doing, it's easy to earn yourself millions of marks (well, lots anyway).

Break Down Questions Into Parts

When you're working out what to write about, underline
the key words in the question so that they <u>stand out</u>.

Here's the <u>instruction</u>.　　　This is the <u>topic</u>.

<u>Choose 3 poems</u> which show feelings about <u>relationships</u>.

Write about the <u>similarities and differences</u> among the texts by comparing:

the feeling in the texts about relationships

<u>how the writers convey these feelings</u> to the reader.

The purple bits are all telling
you <u>what to write about</u>.

You have to follow the <u>instructions</u> in order to get a good grade. If it says "write
about 3 poems", then just writing an answer about 2 of them will lose you marks.

Write About The Same 3 Things In Every Poetry Essay

1 The topic specified by the question
2 Language
3 How the writer wants you to feel

e.g. experience, misunderstanding, strength
and weaknesses, attitudes, feelings, time,
place, thoughts about writing, and so on...

These are all things that will get you points if you write about them.

You'll Always Have to Write About Language

Sometimes questions are obvious —　　How does Simon Armitage use language to create particular effects?

Other times, the question will still <u>want you</u> to write about language, but it'll be worded differently —

These all want you
to write about the
poet's use of language.

Write about how the poets convey (or "show") these feelings to the reader.
Write about the unusual ways in which these ideas are presented.
Write about the ways in which this idea is expressed.

When you are asked to comment on something "<u>interesting</u>", this normally means language too...

Basically, you <u>HAVE</u> to write about the language in every answer,
even if the question <u>doesn't</u> initially seem to be asking you to.

Poetry — wisdom of the soul or just some barmy old pap?...

Once you've understood the question, it's a doddle to start planning your essay. But read the
question through a few times, just to make sure you're not charging off in the wrong direction.

What The Examiner Wants

Poetry's a funny old thing — but there are ways to make it easier.
Shove some of these ideas into your poetry essay, and watch your marks go up.

Always Stick To The Facts

1) Keep on _referring to the text_ in order to back up your argument.

2) Quote a few words at a time, to strengthen your points.

> He implies she was unfaithful by saying she was "Too easily impressed".   **instead of**   He thinks she was unfaithful.

3) Make _positive_ statements, not wishy-washy ones — this will make you sound convincing.

> 'Digging' _is_ a poem about writing poetry.   **instead of**   'Digging' _would seem to be_ a poem about writing poetry.

Comparing Different Poems Will Get You Better Marks

In _comparing_ questions the examiner wants to see that
you can find similarities and differences between poems.

> ...leaves and branches
> Can raise a tragic chorus in a gale
>
> Heaney 'Storm on the Island'

> O let them be left, wildness and wet;
> Long live the weeks and the wilderness yet.
>
> Hopkins 'Inversnaid'

Both of these poems deal with understanding nature. You could say something like...

> While Heaney hears beauty in a big, terrifying storm, Hopkins says that the very wildness of nature is what we should admire and preserve.

DON'T just write about one poem then the other.

You Must Show You Appreciate What the Poet is Doing

To get the top marks you _have_ to _empathise_ with the poet.

> (Empathy)   understanding another person's feelings

So write about how the poet feels and how they want to make _you_ feel.

Be Imaginative

1) A lot of poems deal in hidden meanings and only hint at what they might really be about.

2) This can be irritating, but as far as the exam goes, it's brilliant.

3) It means there are no _right_ or _wrong_ answers, and that _any_ reasonable idea will get you marks.

4) There's only one rule — _you must back up your idea with a quote from the text_.

5) The more creative you are, the better. As long as it's not made up, you _will_ get more marks.

Poems are like suitcases — you need to unpack them...

With poetry, you have to look past the obvious things and search for hidden meanings.
Read each poem at least 3 times, and scribble down any flashes of inspiration you have.

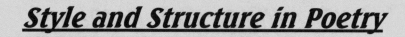

Style and Structure in Poetry

Look at the poem 'as a whole' first. Different structures and styles are chosen for different kinds of poem, and it's worth writing about what you notice...

Learn the Different Types of Poem

There are different types or forms of poems.
Writing about the right form when you spot one, WILL get you extra marks.

Ballads
> They have a regular rhythm and usually tell an epic or dramatic story. They're usually in four-line verses and often have a chorus (e.g. 'The Rime of the Ancient Mariner' or Irish folk songs).

Elegies
> An elegy is written for someone who has died, and is usually quite a slow, thoughtful poem.

Free Verse
> When poems are written in free verse, it means they have lines of irregular length that do not have to rhyme (though some do anyway).

Some poets think it's more like the way people talk, while other poets think it's an excuse to be lazy.

So if the poem is in free verse, you can say: "So-and-so wrote it like this because it's more like the way people talk".

Sonnets
> Sonnets are usually 14 lines long, with a regular rhyme scheme. Popular with Shakespeare himself, and many other traditional writers.

Learn How to Describe the Structure

You've got no excuses for not knowing these words — they're dead easy, and they make you sound ten times more convincing if you use them.

A stanza is the proper word for a verse.

A couplet is a two-line stanza.

A triplet is a three-line stanza.

A quatrain is a four-line stanza (traditionally the most popular).

Work Out The Voice of the Poem

Examiners will be well impressed if you spot the type of narrator, and say how it makes you feel.

You can spot a first-person narrator pretty easily.
They're the ones that use "I" and "me".
Most poetry is written in the first person

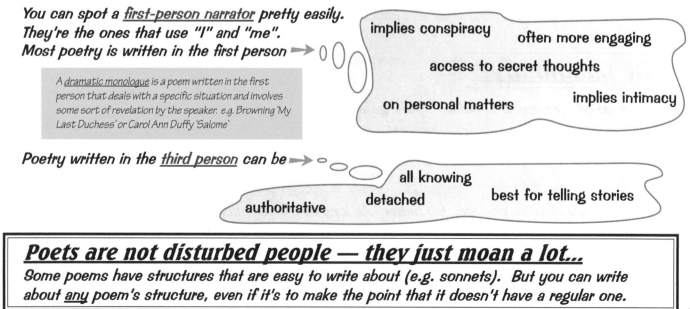

implies conspiracy

often more engaging

access to secret thoughts

on personal matters

implies intimacy

A dramatic monologue is a poem written in the first person that deals with a specific situation and involves some sort of revelation by the speaker. e.g. Browning 'My Last Duchess' or Carol Ann Duffy 'Salome'

Poetry written in the third person can be

all knowing

detached

best for telling stories

authoritative

Poets are not disturbed people — they just moan a lot...

Some poems have structures that are easy to write about (e.g. sonnets). But you can write about any poem's structure, even if it's to make the point that it doesn't have a regular one.

Words To Use When Writing About Poetry

Technical terms are where it's at when it comes to writing about poetry. It'll impress the examiner and get you better marks — but only if you use the power wisely.

Using the Right Technical Words Will Get You Marks

Don't use these words if you're unsure what they mean,
but you've really got no excuses for not knowing them by now...

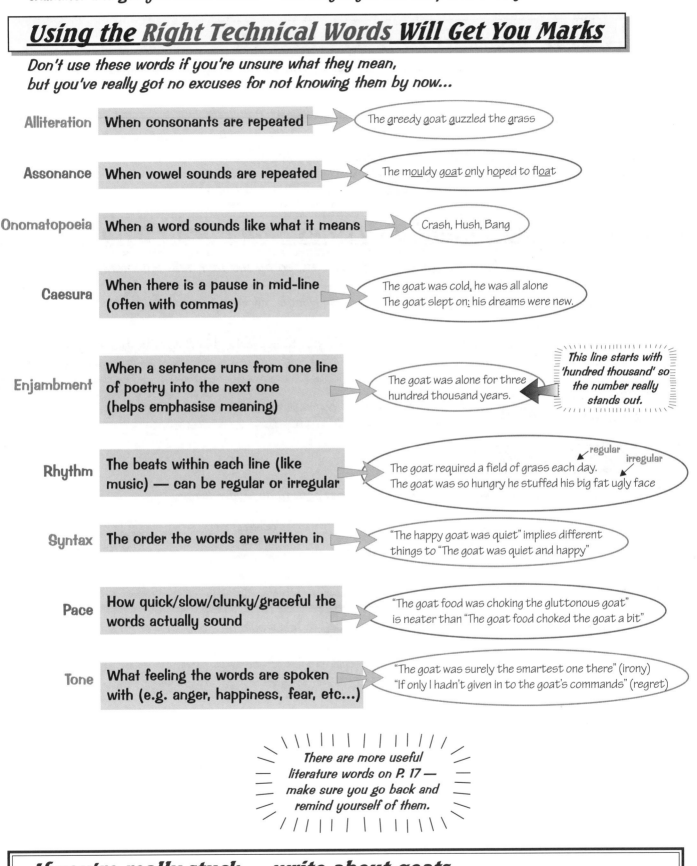

Alliteration — When consonants are repeated → The greedy goat guzzled the grass

Assonance — When vowel sounds are repeated → The mouldy goat only hoped to float

Onomatopoeia — When a word sounds like what it means → Crash, Hush, Bang

Caesura — When there is a pause in mid-line (often with commas) → The goat was cold, he was all alone
The goat slept on: his dreams were new.

Enjambment — When a sentence runs from one line of poetry into the next one (helps emphasise meaning) → The goat was alone for three hundred thousand years.
This line starts with 'hundred thousand' so the number really stands out.

Rhythm — The beats within each line (like music) — can be regular or irregular → The goat required a field of grass each day. *(regular)*
The goat was so hungry he stuffed his big fat ugly face *(irregular)*

Syntax — The order the words are written in → "The happy goat was quiet" implies different things to "The goat was quiet and happy"

Pace — How quick/slow/clunky/graceful the words actually sound → "The goat food was choking the gluttonous goat" is neater than "The goat food choked the goat a bit"

Tone — What feeling the words are spoken with (e.g. anger, happiness, fear, etc...) → "The goat was surely the smartest one there" (irony)
"If only I hadn't given in to the goat's commands" (regret)

There are more useful literature words on P. 17 — make sure you go back and remind yourself of them.

If you're really stuck — write about goats...

Remember... you're trying to show that you know how to <u>use</u> these technical terms, not just that you've heard of them. Don't go slinging them in because you think they look nice.

What The Examiner Wants

No, I'm afraid this page isn't about a sequel to that __great__ Mel Gibson film,
it's about things you can do to __impress__ the examiner in... err well, the exam.*

* What Women Want, 2001
Mel Gibson, Helen Hunt.

Write a Bit About When it was Written

1) You must show you know __when__ the text was written and published, and what significance this has.

2) Some books are set in the same period they were written in.
Other books are set in a __different__ period from the one they were __published__ in.

3) This means the author can write about present day issues without criticising anyone openly.

> *George Orwell wrote Animal Farm in 1945. It tells the story of a bunch of pigs who take over a farm. It's not actually about pigs though — it's an allegory about events which took place around that time in Communist Russia.*

Show You Understand the Issues Being Dealt With

Show the examiner that there are __wider issues__ being raised by the text, and comment on them.

Texts can have __social__ implications.   →   *Robin Hood is concerned with poverty.*

They can have __historical__ implications.   →   *Different versions of Robin Hood have different interpretations of the role the royals played at that time.*

They can have moral or __philosophical__ implications.   →   *Robin Hood basically condones theft and mugging.*

Write in Detail

Most questions ask you to comment on how a writer has __shown__ the reader things.

- **Personality of a character**
- **Experiences of characters**
- **Attitudes of characters**
- **Conflicts between characters**
- **Message and meaning of the text as a whole**

You have to answer in detail —

> Write about how Dickens shows us the changes in Scrooge's character.

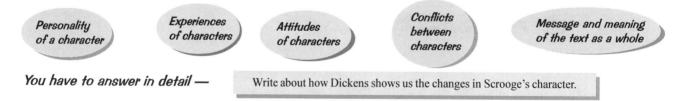

> Chapter 23 comes after chapter 22 but before chapter 24.

This would be a bad answer. It's too general.

> Scrooge's return to reality needs to be urgent and vivid. Dickens precedes it with the scene where Scrooge forsees his own funeral, making sure that the return to life has a great impact, as it is shown just after death.

This is much better.

Try to Be Original

If something occurs to you while you're reading the text (about language, a character, __anything__), then say it in your essay — even (and especially) if you've never been taught it.

> You need a quote to back it up.
> It must be relevant to the question you're answering.

Any __reasonable__ observation will impress the examiner and get you better marks.

Originality is the soul of wit — who said that again...

Learn all the stuff on this page. It's there to help you.   *Then relax, take the evening off. Maybe rent a video ... a Mel Gibson movie...*

What The Examiner Wants

The main thing is to <u>read</u> the question carefully, so you don't go barking up the wrong tree.

Questions About the Message Can Look Scary

Don't get scared by questions that ask about the overall message of the text.

As long as you cover your back with <u>quotes</u> and <u>details</u> from the text, you'll be just fine.

This is the kind of question you might get:

Here's the <u>topic</u> you need to write about.

> What do you think are the main <u>reasons for the change from friendship to violence</u> in *Lord of the Flies*, and <u>what is the writer trying to show by this change</u>?

This is the <u>message</u> bit.

In questions about the message, you <u>always</u> need to write about <u>what the writer is trying to say</u>.

> Golding suggests in *Lord of the Flies* that all of us are capable of degenerating into violence when cut off from society. We can tell this because...

Some Questions Talk About a Specific Chunk of Text

Some questions will quote a page or so of one of your set texts and ask you to <u>respond</u> to it.

These can be easier to answer, as you've got the text in front of you to quote from, and also because <u>you'll recognise it</u> from the book (I hope).

BUT — just because the text is right there, it doesn't mean you're allowed to be lazy.

Above all, answer these 3 questions:

...and now my hair is as thick as ever. Thank you CGP.

> What is the extract's relevance to the rest of the text?
> Why is it important?
> What implications does it have for the text as a whole?

You Might Have to Write About Style

Some questions will ask you specifically about the writing style.

Your answer will be about the usual style things (e.g. language, imagery, style, tone — see P. 16). Remember — don't talk about these things impersonally, as if they just happen by accident.

Let the examiner know that you understand it's <u>all done by the writer</u> — that the story doesn't just write itself. It really is the key to better marks.

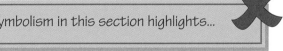

The symbolism in this section highlights...

The <u>writer uses</u> symbolism in this section in order to highlight...

The writer puts a bad joke at the bottom of each page to annoy the reader...

The examiners really want to know that you understand that stories are made up by a real human being. Quite silly, isn't it? You'd think they'd already have figured that one out themselves...

Some Tips About the Writer

Oh, it's so confusing, but here's a tip — don't trust narrators. Too many end up being untruthful.

You Need to Ask Yourself Questions About the Writing

Some questions ask you to think about how the writer communicates with the reader.

How Does the Writer Put the Text Together?

Paragraph structure ⟶ how meaning is revealed from sentence to sentence.

Book structure ⟶ if the book is split into chapters, how this affects the reader.

With language ⟶ implications and what is left unsaid.

Through the narrator ⟶ how the story is told.

With imagery ⟶ how emotions and scenes are built up.

Why Does the Writer Choose One Way Over Another?

It's what writing is all about — finding the best way to tell your story.
There's no right or wrong way — it's just about finding what's appropriate.

Irvine Welsh wrote *Trainspotting* in Scottish dialect, as this was appropriate to the book's main characters.

Kurt Vonnegut wrote *Cat's Cradle* in very short sections. This is appropriate to the way the facts are uncovered slowly and in pieces by the main character.

Show You Understand How the Writer Does It

1) The examiner wants to know that you understand that short stories and novels have been <u>thought up</u>, <u>manipulated</u> and <u>written</u> by the writer.

2) You can show that you are aware of this in a very simple way — by referring to the writer.

In "Your Shoes", the author Michèle Roberts shows us only the mother's side of the story. This means our understanding of what happened isn't complete.

The Narrator is NOT The Writer

1) It can be tempting to think that the voice telling the story is the voice of the actual writer.

2) BUT — this is totally wrong. You must remember that the narrator is <u>created</u> by the writer in order to tell the story.

3) They know as much or as little as the <u>writer</u> wants them to know.

4) So, make sure you refer to the writer, to show you understand how books are put together — something like "The <u>writer uses the narrator...</u>" NOT "The <u>narrator says...</u>".

The narrator is not the writer, but he's always called Dave...

Ours is not to reason why, ours is but to do exams then go home for a nice brew. Examiners want you to show that you know about writers as well as the stuff they write. They don't want much...

Questions About Characters

It's not that hard to gather a heap of information about particular characters. If you do, it means you'll have a much better chance of getting to the heart of an exam question quickly and efficiently.

Character Questions Are the Examiner's *Favourite*

Questions about characters are the most <u>popular</u>.

It's pretty obvious why, really — characters act out the story, and <u>shape the plot</u>. Their actions and experiences are what stories are all about — they come into everything. You need to be able to write about them <u>confidently</u> if you want to get good marks.

Make Sure You *Prepare* For Character Questions

Make <u>revision notes</u> on these things for the texts you're studying — then you'll be sorted for any exam question on characters. Not all of these will apply to all stories — pick the ones that fit best.

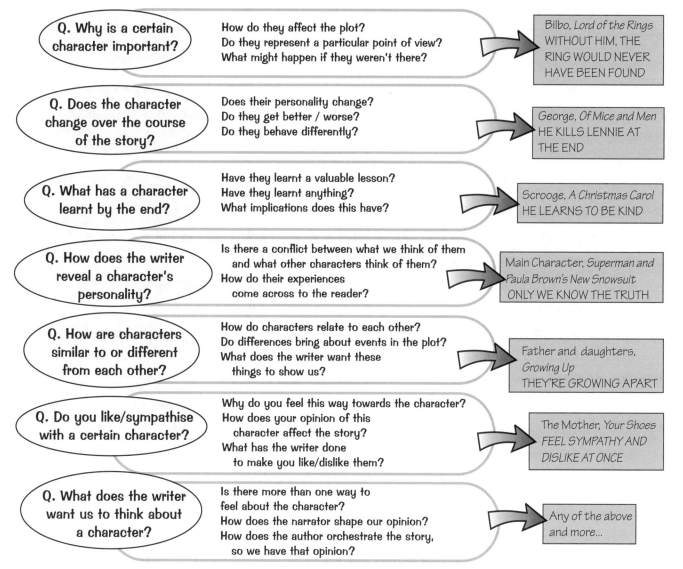

Q. Why is a certain character important?
How do they affect the plot?
Do they represent a particular point of view?
What might happen if they weren't there?
→ *Bilbo, Lord of the Rings* WITHOUT HIM, THE RING WOULD NEVER HAVE BEEN FOUND

Q. Does the character change over the course of the story?
Does their personality change?
Do they get better / worse?
Do they behave differently?
→ *George, Of Mice and Men* HE KILLS LENNIE AT THE END

Q. What has a character learnt by the end?
Have they learnt a valuable lesson?
Have they learnt anything?
What implications does this have?
→ *Scrooge, A Christmas Carol* HE LEARNS TO BE KIND

Q. How does the writer reveal a character's personality?
Is there a conflict between what we think of them and what other characters think of them?
How do their experiences come across to the reader?
→ *Main Character, Superman and Paula Brown's New Snowsuit* ONLY WE KNOW THE TRUTH

Q. How are characters similar to or different from each other?
How do characters relate to each other?
Do differences bring about events in the plot?
What does the writer want these things to show us?
→ *Father and daughters, Growing Up* THEY'RE GROWING APART

Q. Do you like/sympathise with a certain character?
Why do you feel this way towards the character?
How does your opinion of this character affect the story?
What has the writer done to make you like/dislike them?
→ *The Mother, Your Shoes* FEEL SYMPATHY AND DISLIKE AT ONCE

Q. What does the writer want us to think about a character?
Is there more than one way to feel about the character?
How does the narrator shape our opinion?
How does the author orchestrate the story, so we have that opinion?
→ *Any of the above and more...*

This <u>ISN'T</u> so you can pre-plan essays — that's ridiculous. You can't tell what the questions will be. It's just so that you've prepared the background, and have the best possible chance.

Yaaaaaaaaaaaaaaaaaaaaawn —this is exhausting stuff...

Well at least this is the last page of the section. And look, I've even brought you a nice comfy bed so you can have a quick nap before continuing.

Revision Summary

Woah, that's another three sections under your belt. If you can remember the big areas you have to include when you do each kind of essay, that's a good start. But you do have to go into a bit of depth and detail to score the good marks. Get your teeth into these questions and make sure you know your stuff. Once you're getting 'em all right you'll have what these examiners want in your head — ready to let rip in the exam...

<u>Drama</u>

1) You're writing about a play. Give four examples of things you can do to impress the examiner.

2) Explain three major issues that a play might deal with.

3) Explain the difference between a tragedy and a comedy.

4) What is dialogue?
   a) A character speaking their thoughts aloud
   b) One character talking to another
   c) A character talking to the moon

5) What are stage directions? What is the point of giving them?

6) What does personification mean?

7) What is stagecraft? What things should you talk about to show that you appreciate it?

8) How old are Shakespeare's plays? Explain two things about them that are old-fashioned.

9) What's the difference between poetic verse and blank verse?

<u>Poetry</u>

1) What three areas should you write about in every poetry essay?

2) Explain two ways of making your argument convincing.

3) How do you show you appreciate what a poet is trying to do (and get the top marks)?

4) Describe the four different forms of poem.

5) What is: a) a stanza?   b) a couplet?   c) a triplet?   d) a quatrain?

6) Explain three effects that a poem with a first-person narrator can put across.

7) List the nine different technical terms that you can use to talk about poetry. Write a line to explain what each one means.

<u>Stories and Novels</u>

1) When writing about a text, what four things should you do to thrill the examiner?

2) How does an author put a text together? Name the five things they use.

3) Who is the narrator?
   a) The author
   b) Someone created by the author
   c) Someone created in a laboratory

4) Write down five questions you could ask about characters to prepare yourself for the exam.

5) What are the two vital things you should include when writing about the message of a text?

6) What three questions should you ask when you're faced with a specific chunk of text?

7) What should you make clear when talking about the writing style?
   a) That it is all done by the writer
   b) That the book wrote itself
   c) That you couldn't give a monkeys

Structure Your Essay

You <u>know</u> you're right — you just have to persuade <u>everyone else</u> you're right.
You need a good argument and truckloads of evidence or no one's going to believe you.

Keep your Essay <u>Structured</u>

To get a good grade your essay needs to be:

<u>COHERENT</u>: *easy to follow, consistent, smooth-flowing*
<u>LOGICAL</u>: *well-reasoned, realistic*
<u>PERSUASIVE</u>: *convinces readers*

To achieve this you need a <u>clear structure</u>.

1) <u>Work out a plan</u> — *decide on your main points, then spend about five minutes using them to form a plan like the one below. A plan will help organise your thinking into paragraphs. You need to write in paragraphs to get grade C or above.*

2) <u>Don't keep repeating the same idea</u> — *organise your essay into 3 or 4 key ideas and use your plan to put them in order.*

3) <u>Fill in the gaps</u> — *once you've got a plan you can see where to fit in bits of evidence, facts, opinions, etc. and where you need more ammunition.*

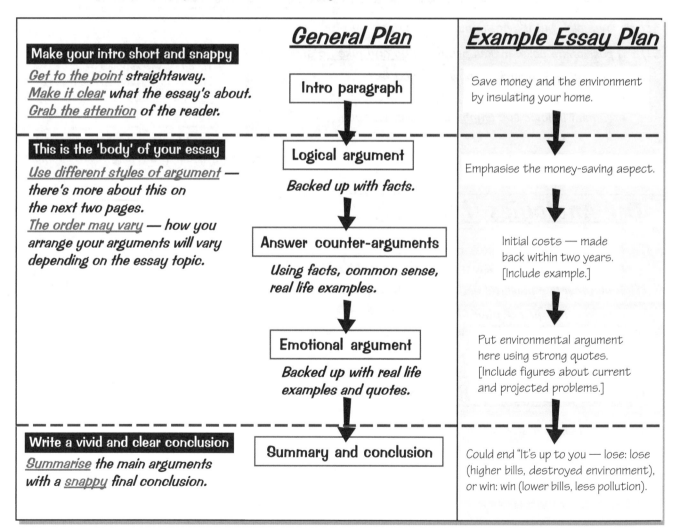

Make your intro short and snappy

<u>Get to the point</u> *straightaway.*
<u>Make it clear</u> *what the essay's about.*
<u>Grab the attention</u> *of the reader.*

This is the 'body' of your essay

<u>Use different styles of argument</u> — *there's more about this on the next two pages.*
<u>The order may vary</u> — *how you arrange your arguments will vary depending on the essay topic.*

Write a vivid and clear conclusion

<u>Summarise</u> *the main arguments with a <u>snappy</u> final conclusion.*

General Plan

Intro paragraph

Logical argument
Backed up with facts.

Answer counter-arguments
Using facts, common sense, real life examples.

Emotional argument
Backed up with real life examples and quotes.

Summary and conclusion

Example Essay Plan

Save money and the environment by insulating your home.

Emphasise the money-saving aspect.

Initial costs — made back within two years. [Include example.]

Put environmental argument here using strong quotes. [Include figures about current and projected problems.]

Could end "It's up to you — lose: lose (higher bills, destroyed environment), or win: win (lower bills, less pollution).

I love it when a plan comes together...

Plan what to write and write what you planned. Then there's no way that your essay can stray off the point. Which reminds me, did you see Eastenders last night? I cooked a nice stew as well.

Setting Up Your Argument

Here are all the <u>cunning tricks</u> you can use to make your essay <u>persuasive</u> — logic, emotion, analogy and ethical beliefs. Throw in a little deceit and megalomania and you're ready for politics...

Use Logical Reasoning

You won't begin to impress the examiners unless your argument is <u>logical</u>.

1) Show the reader that your argument provides the <u>only logical position</u>.

2) Use <u>definite</u> language (e.g. 'will', 'all', 'definitely') rather than <u>vague</u> language (e.g 'might', 'some', 'possibly') — it makes you sound more confident.

3) <u>Check your reasoning</u>. If it's flawed, your argument fails.

✓ If you want our farm animals to be treated humanely and raised organically, becoming vegetarian isn't the answer. Choosing to eat meat from organic and humane farms will promote this kind of farming and put pressure on stores to stock more of these brands...

Definite language and a logical argument makes this point convincing.

Add Emotion to the Logic to Build your Argument

Logic is crucial, but it's not enough on its own.

1) A passionate belief makes people <u>sit up and take note</u>.

2) Use <u>striking</u> language to show how you feel.

3) Don't rely on emotion alone. Always base your argument in logic and <u>emphasise</u> it with emotion.

There is no time left for mulling things over. If we don't act now our river ecosystem will be destroyed. It will be nothing more than <u>polluted sludge</u>, littered with the <u>rotting carcasses</u> of an ecosystem that took <u>thousands of years to establish</u>...

This emotional language makes you feel <u>guilty</u> about destroying the environment.

Use Analogies if they Fit

1) Use analogies if the idea is complex. They help readers to grasp the basic argument using <u>simple ideas</u>.

2) They provide a powerful and <u>memorable</u> image.

3) <u>Don't</u> try to squeeze your idea into an analogy. Only use an analogy if it's useful to explain your point.

These new statistics just conceal the problems without solving them. It's like trying to ignore a river by building a dam. The water, like the problems, will just build and build...

Dam...

This analogy helps the reader <u>understand</u> the buildup of problems.

Include Ethical Beliefs

1) Ethical beliefs are commonly held beliefs about things that are <u>right and wrong</u>, e.g. 'poverty is bad' and 'freedom of speech is good'.

2) Use them to give your argument an <u>ethical perspective</u>.

Giving aid to poor nations is not enough. In many cases debt is crippling their economies, keeping 80% of the population below the poverty line. We should also cancel all their debts.

You don't actually need to say 'poverty is wrong'. People already know that.

Logic — I pink therefore I ham...

Tug at people's <u>heartstrings</u> and they'll be <u>putty</u> in your hands. It's the <u>oldest trick</u> in the book. But don't get <u>carried away</u> — the moment you stop being realistic, that's when you've lost 'em.

Supporting Your Argument

You get <u>marked</u> on <u>how well</u> you've <u>backed up</u> your argument. And now that you know that, there's <u>no excuse</u> for not researching your essays — especially in your coursework.

Use Facts Carefully

1)   Don't get bogged down in <u>complicated statistics</u>.

2)   Use <u>simple</u>, easy-to-understand facts.

3)   Keep figures to a minimum — but make sure you <u>don't</u> alter what they mean.

> ✗ Using the Keyword method, word retrieval increased by 16% with a mean improvement of 36 words (and a standard deviation of 8).

Confusing — too much detail.

> 36 more words were recalled on average when the Keyword method was used. ✓

This is a good statistic, because it's easy to understand.

Use Opinions from Experts

1)   Use expert opinion to give <u>backing</u> to your arguments.

2)   Say <u>who</u> they are and <u>how</u> they're related to your argument.

3)   You can include opinion as <u>quotes</u> (see example below) or <u>part of the text</u> (see example above).

Use Relevant Quotations

> Chief Medical Officer Robert Thial agrees, saying, "I've investigated each method of execution and they all cause unnecessary pain and suffering".

1)   Use good quotes to provide <u>sound bites</u> that stick in people's minds.

2)   Don't just stick in a quote for the sake of it: make sure it's <u>relevant</u>.

3)   Keep it short. <u>Don't</u> include long extracts.

4)   Use <u>quotation marks</u> and also say <u>who</u> you're quoting — otherwise you won't get the marks for using the quotation

5)   <u>Never</u> make up quotes, or alter existing ones. It's the same as lying.

Use Real-life Examples

1)   Your argument should sound as though it's true in <u>real-life</u> terms, not groundless theory.

2)   Give real-life examples to provide your argument with cold, hard <u>reality</u>.

3)   Choose examples that fit your argument as <u>closely</u> as possible. If the connection is weak don't use it.

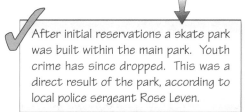

> ✓ After initial reservations a skate park was built within the main park. Youth crime has since dropped. This was a direct result of the park, according to local police sergeant Rose Leven.

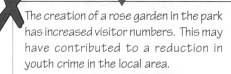

> ✗ The creation of a rose garden in the park has increased visitor numbers. This may have contributed to a reduction in youth crime in the local area.

I know it's true — I made it up myself...

Facts, examples, opinions and quotes all <u>add punch</u> to your argument — but don't overdo it.
<u>Good rule of thumb</u>: use one <u>well chosen</u> piece of evidence for <u>each part</u> of the argument.

Persuasive Writing Tools

To get an <u>A grade</u> your essay really has to be persuasive — here's <u>four handy tips</u> to help you.

Keep Your Writing <u>Polite</u> and <u>Non-aggressive</u>

1) Being polite is very important when you're writing about people with the <u>opposite opinion</u> to yours.

2) You should criticise their <u>opinions</u> only. Don't criticise them personally — you'll lose marks for being rude.

3) If it sounds like a <u>personal attack</u> it will make you sound angry, and it won't help you persuade anyone.

> ✗ A lot of people think school uniforms make everyone equal. They are wrong...

> ✓ It is often said that school uniforms make everyone equal. This isn't true...

Make Your <u>Positive</u> Points <u>Personal</u>

You need to make the readers feel that you're all on the <u>same side</u>.

> <u>We</u> all believe that individuality is important. ◄ The "<u>we</u>" makes it sound as if your readers <u>agree</u> with you already.

You can also use "<u>you</u>" to talk <u>directly</u> to your readers, especially if you're trying to persuade them to do something. It's as if you're trying to persuade them personally.

> Giving blood saves lives. As a compassionate person, do you really need to read further before you take action?

Use <u>Rhetorical Questions</u> To Make Your Points

1) A <u>rhetorical question</u> is a question that requires no answer — the answer should be obvious from the text. It's used for effect.

> Is this sort of thing acceptable in our society?

2) It's a brilliant trick that writers and politicians use all the time — and the <u>examiners</u> will be looking out for it too. Leaving the readers to put the answer together themselves is a great way of making them <u>agree with you</u>.

Use language like "ruining the countryside" to <u>emphasise</u> your opinion.

> Can anyone tell me why road builders are <u>ruining the countryside</u>?

Keep Your Writing Punchy with <u>Magic Threes</u>

It's one of the <u>easiest</u> and most useful tricks for <u>emphasising</u> your points.
Instead of just using one describing-word in a sentence, use <u>three</u>.

> The development of a European single policy is an expensive, time-consuming, and unworkable nightmare.

The Good, the Bad and the Dopey
Starring Beano Reeves, Goldie Woopsberg and Demi A. Favour.
Directed by Tinfin Quarantino. Filmed in Crumby-gag-o-vision.

This sounds <u>much better</u> than "A European single policy is expensive and unworkable". It's a trick you'll hear <u>politicians</u> using in speeches — it <u>stresses</u> the points you're making.

Can I write rhetorical questions?

What a fantastic page. <u>Four ways</u> of making your writing as punchy as a <u>boxing octopus</u>. And on top of that, anyone reading it will be <u>convinced</u> that what you're saying is <u>completely true</u>.

Think About Your Readers

There's no point writing something down if nobody's going to bother reading it. Write your essay from your reader's point of view and grab yourself some juicy marks while you're at it.

Put Yourself in the Reader's Shoes

1) Any piece of writing is designed to be <u>read</u> by someone — so you should <u>suit</u> your writing to the reader.

2) That means trying to <u>second-guess</u> what a reader's reactions might be.

Identify Readers' Concerns and Address Them

Think about <u>concerns</u> the reader might have, and then:

1) Make their concerns sound like <u>understandable reactions</u>.

2) Let them know that you've <u>thought</u> about these concerns.

3) <u>Tell them</u> how your argument addresses the concerns.

> A concern that many residents may have is the question of litter after the concert. Cleaning up quickly is of the utmost importance to us. To do this there will be a twenty-strong team working quietly through the night to clear it by 6:00am the next day.

Imagine Counter-Arguments and Argue Against Them

A good way of persuading people is to imagine how they would argue against you, and answer their points. Imagine you're writing to persuade the RSPCA to let you work for them...

First think up all the arguments <u>against</u> your opinion.

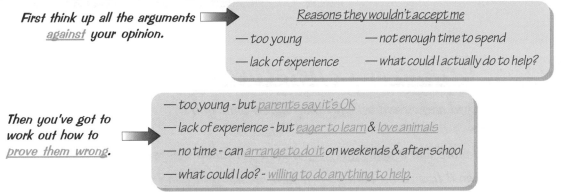

> *Reasons they wouldn't accept me*
> — too young   — not enough time to spend
> — lack of experience   — what could I actually do to help?

Then you've got to work out how to <u>prove them wrong</u>.

> — too young - but <u>parents say it's OK</u>
> — lack of experience - but <u>eager to learn</u> & <u>love animals</u>
> — no time - can <u>arrange to do it</u> on weekends & after school
> — what could I do? - <u>willing to do anything to help</u>.

Challenge Biases and Expectations

Q: How do you persuade a reader who will have <u>biases</u> that make them automatically disagree?

A: With difficulty. Here are some tips to make it easier though:

1) Your first paragraph is <u>crucial</u> — you've got to keep them reading — it needs <u>impact</u> and interesting ideas that make them want to keep reading.

2) <u>Don't</u> disguise your argument and don't say things you disagree with. If you do, your argument will sound <u>weak</u> and you'll sound as if you don't believe in what you're saying.

3) <u>Challenge expectations</u> — come at the issue from a different <u>point of view</u> than the one they're expecting.

<u>Me? Automatically disagree? Absolutely not...</u>

<u>REMEMBER</u> — <u>think</u> like your reader and you'll always be <u>one step ahead</u> of them. Which means they'll be <u>easier</u> to <u>bend to your will</u>.... AHA HA HA HA... AHA HA HA... [diabolical laughter]

Analyse, Review and Comment

"Analyse, Review and Comment" — yawn. Yep, this is <u>boring</u>, but it's pretty <u>easy</u> so stick with it. It's a bit more clinical than an arguing essay — like a report. So leave out the <u>emotional</u> stuff.

You Still Have to be Convincing

1) 'Analyse' and 'review' might sound like vague and fluffy words. But they're not.

2) They still mean you have to be <u>clear</u>, <u>logical</u> and <u>precise</u>.

3) The examiner wants you to sound as though you know what you're talking about.

4) You have to write <u>convincingly</u>.

> Q1. Analyse the relative merits and disadvantages of Jedi and Wizards.

<u>Analyse</u> — break the subject down into pieces and look at each one individually.

> Wizards have staffs, pointy hats, long beards, and cool eyebrows.
> Jedi have mind-control powers, light sabers and a vague sense of irony.

<u>Review</u> — bring them all together again, with an overview of the whole topic.

> Jedi seem to be more powerful than Wizards, although Wizards have longer beards.

<u>Comment</u> — Make a balanced comment on the arguments you've discussed in your essay.

> Of course, neither Jedi nor Wizards would be any good as chat-show hosts...

Make Your Writing More Detached

1) You're still trying to show readers <u>why</u> they agree with you
   — the difference is that you have to sound <u>detached</u>.

2) It needs to read more like a <u>clinical report</u> than a persuasive essay.

3) That doesn't mean it has to be boring — it just means <u>you can't take sides</u>.

Make Sure You Plan All Sides of the Argument

You're presenting a report on <u>all the different sides</u> of an argument.

The whole point is to make it all as <u>concise</u> and orderly as possible.

Planning an analysis essay needs <u>bullet points</u>.

Wizards	Jedi
• hats	• mind control
• beards	• light sabers
• staffs	• sense of irony
• eyebrows	• not good at parties
• gravelly voices	• family troubles

Analysis — the best way to destroy a psychology student...

I knew a guy who was a psychology student. He always used to sit in silence staring at people, stroking his chin, trying to freak them out. I wonder whatever happened to him...

Making Your Analysis Sound Good

Here are the tricks for sounding authoritative and impartial. They're easy to learn — and once you've got it, you can set about making people believe pretty much anything. Politicians do it all the time.

Never Use "I" or "You"

So long, and thanks for all the pot noodles

1) While the first person ("I...") is useful for making fiction sound believable, it's useless for trying to make your own real opinions sound credible.

2) Using "I" sounds like it's just your personal, unimportant opinion.

3) Using the third person ("It") sounds more detached, professional and authoritative.

I have noticed that the temperature in swimming pool water has been rising for the last 3 months. — bad

The temperature of swimming pool water has been rising over the last 3 months. — good

Keep it Simple

1) On no account get carried away in an analysis essay.

2) They're not the same as arguing essays — they have to be detached and impartial.

3) Don't use analogies and emotional pleas. They won't sound believable.

4) Just write your points simply and clearly. e.g. 'Vegetarians are not universally respected' NOT 'Vegetarians get laughed at by bloodthirsty meat-eating scoundrels on a daily basis'.

Your Essay Could Be About the Pros and Cons

Structuring your essay around good and bad points of the topic keeps your essay focused.

This is the analysis part of the essay. →

Essay plan

Intro — about vegetarians

Pros and cons of vegetarianism

Review — good: idealistic points;   bad: practical points

Comment — should ask whether you would rather be idealistic or practical

There are 2 different ways of writing about pros and cons:

Make 3 points IN FAVOUR of something...
... then make 3 points AGAINST it.

or: Analyse good and bad together, putting your points coherently, in a logical order.

Good — moral, personal, good for environment

Bad   — unhealthy, inconvenient, anti-social

Point 1 — it's moral, but can be unhealthy

Point 2 — it's a strong personal choice, but it can be inconvenient for shopping and eating out

Point 3 — it's good for the environment but some people see it as being anti-social

It doesn't really matter which approach you use, just make it sound clear and professional.

Frankly my dear — I don't give a pair of dingo's kidneys...

It's a shame when someone's got a great argument that makes you think "hang on, they might be onto something" — then they spoil it by going off on one and losing the thread of the point of the...

Finishing Your Essay

Finish off with a <u>clear conclusion</u> and then <u>check</u> your work.

End With A Clear Conclusion

Start by <u>summing up</u> all the <u>key</u> points.

> To sum up, banning cars on the road during school hours is not practical. There are too many businesses and homes nearby. Reducing the speed limit is a good idea, as long as it is properly enforced. This could definitely be helped by putting in speed bumps as a form of traffic control.
>
> Even though traffic all around the town would be affected, the second and third plans are worth putting into practice. They could save a child's life.

Based on the <u>whole</u> report, say what <u>you think</u> should be done and <u>why</u>.

Leave Enough Time For A Proper Ending

This may sound stupid, but in an exam situation it's surprisingly easy to <u>run out</u> of time. You've <u>got to leave</u> enough time to <u>finish</u> your essay properly — with a <u>clear ending</u>.

Give yourself <u>at least five minutes</u>
to write a <u>conclusion</u> for your essay.

Look Over the Essay — 3 Final Checks

Leave at least <u>five minutes</u>, at the end, for checking your work.

Check your ARGUMENT/ADVICE   clear, no waffle, well-structured, all points covered

Check your ENGLISH   spelling, punctuation, paragraphs, style, language

Check the DETAILS   accurate quotes, accurate figures

Let's conclude this argument — outside, now...

I know, you've heard this all before. I'm only banging on so much about the conclusion because it's important — it's the bit they're left remembering. You <u>must</u> always leave room for a good en...

Revision Summary

Arguing skills and analysing skills are really important — you'll end up using the same techniques for loads of different essays in the exam and in your coursework. In a way they're quite an easy sort of essay to get to grips with — factual, clinical and (mostly) detached. Kind of like Science really. Anyway, make sure you can do all these questions, and that way you won't be telling Jerry Springer in 10 years' time about how you failed English and wished you'd worked harder...

Arguing and Analysing

1) What is an 'arguing and analysing' essay trying to achieve?

2) Why is it important to be logical in your thinking?

3) Write a brief essay plan in response to the following question — "Should you try to get good grades in your GCSEs?" (use p.33 as a guide if you don't remember properly).

4) Explain why structuring your essay is important.

5) What's an analogy and why are analogies effective?

6) Why is it important to support your argument with facts?

7) Explain why it's better to use simple facts rather than complicated statistics.

8) Which of these quotes would be appropriate in an essay on getting good grades, and why?

   a) "All teachers are fascists" (source: unknown)

   b) "Most University Admissions staff look at how well students did in their GCSEs" (Prof. J. Morgan: University of Leeds, 2002)

9) Why are real-life examples more effective than fictional ones?

10) Explain why you need to keep your writing style polite and non-aggressive.

11) Why do you want your reader to feel as if you're on the same side as them?

12) What is a rhetorical question and why are rhetorical questions effective?

13) Should your points be a) punchy, b) lengthy or c) gravy?

14) Do you need to try to put yourself in the reader's shoes when writing your essay? Why?

15) Why should you address any concerns you think your reader might have about your argument?

Analyse, Review, Comment

16) Why should an 'analyse, review and comment' essay be more clinical than an arguing essay?

17) Should your writing be a) clear, b) logical, c) precise or d) all of the above?

18) Why should you try to cover all the different sides of an argument in your essay?

19) Explain why using the first person ("I") is not appropriate for this type of essay.

20) Read this question, then answer parts a) and b) — "Analyse the state of the current top 40".
    a) Write an essay plan where you discuss the good and bad points separately (as on p.39).
    b) Write an essay plan where you discuss the good and bad points simultaneously (also on p.39).

21) Is either one of the two suggested essay plans from Q.20, better than the other?

22) Explain why your essay needs a conclusion.

23) Which of the following things should you check for at the end of the exam?
    a) clarity of argument   b) proper use of English
    c) use of details and facts   d) integrity of metatarsals

Getting Your Answer Right

In the exam, you'll have to do a question where you need to either <u>inform</u>, <u>explain</u> or <u>describe</u>. Each type needs to be tackled in a different way — and you'll lose marks if you don't do it right.

Pick out the Key Words in the Question

To answer any question well, you need a clear idea of:

1) Your <u>purpose</u> — What are you writing about? And do you need to inform, explain or describe?
2) Your <u>audience</u> — The tone, structure and words you choose will depend on who your reader is.

<u>Key words</u> in the question will tell you what sort of answer the examiner is after.
Scribble a circle around them and keep them in mind as you write:

Q1. There are many pressures on young people today. Explain what you think are the main pressures and how they affect your life and the lives of people you know.

Q2. Write an article describing an ideal holiday place. It could be somewhere you have been to, or an imaginary destination.

Q3. Write an informative article for teachers about 'Clothes and Today's Teenager'.

Informing is about Giving Information to Your Reader

For this type of question, imagine you're teaching your reader something that they don't know much about. You want to give them a good outline of the topic so they can understand it better.

Whether you're writing to inform or explain, it's dead important to go into detail and back up your statements with <u>evidence</u>. An essay that is just personal opinion will get you zilch marks. Give <u>examples</u> every time you make a <u>statement</u>, to explain what you are saying. There are two ways to do this:

Give an <u>example/fact</u>.
Give an <u>expert's opinion</u>.

STATEMENT

Smoking is really bad for your health.

EXAMPLE/FACT

- For example, smoking is one cause of cancer and heart disease.
- A link was found between lung cancer and smoking in 1950.

EXPERT OPINION

- The scientist Geraldine Hunt writes that smoking is "a vicious killer."

Explaining Means Giving a Detailed Discussion

You might be asked to explain what you think about something.
You need to explain what your beliefs are, in a <u>logical way</u>:

Decide what your main arguments are, then write a paragraph explaining each one.
Make sure that each point is backed up with evidence — reasons why you think what you say.

Make Descriptions In-depth and Interesting

When you answer a describing question, it's all about giving a <u>variety</u> of <u>interesting detail</u>. Entertain your reader by using loads of <u>unusual</u> and <u>exciting</u> words and <u>different kinds of sentences</u>. Describe <u>sensations</u> and <u>feelings</u> to give them a picture of what you're describing, in their mind's eye.

The beach is yellow and the sun is really hot. You can order drinks whenever you want.

ADD DEPTH *+ INTEREST*

The sun's bright rays sparkle down on the golden sand dunes, where you can sprawl out while a handsome waiter fetches you ice-cold cocktails.

Giving good descriptions — the proof is in the paragraph...

Paragraphs... I'll say that again... PARAGRAPHS. It's an easy way to organise your essay but it'll get you good marks. Each paragraph should be a statement, followed by evidence to back it up.

Starting Your Essay

As I said, in your exam you'll have to write an essay that explains, informs or describes. No one's trying to trick you — it really should be pretty simple, as long as you know what you're doing.

5 Ways Not to Muck Up

1) _Write About What You Know_

If you have a _choice of topics_ you should always choose one you _know a lot about_.
For example, a question might ask you to describe how to look after a pet.
You should choose a pet your family or friend owns, because you'll know more to write about.

2) _Scribble Down a Plan_

Note down the things you need to cover.

It'll make sure you cover all the points and do it in a _logical order_.

That'll make it much easier for the reader to understand what you are writing about.

You should spend _5 minutes_ on the plan.

> Question:
> _Write an essay to explain how to do an everyday task_
>
> Task selected:
> To explain how to make dinner.
>
> Plan:
> Introduction
> What to eat (how to decide)
> How to cook it (reading labels, etc.)
> How to serve the food / eat it...
> Conclusion

The stages are listed in a clear order...

3) _Write an Introduction_

Start the essay with an _introduction_ to say what the essay is going to be about.

This should give the reader an idea of how you are going to _tackle the topic_.

> Introduction:
> Cooking dinner is one of the most useful things you can learn — it's cheaper and usually healthier than eating out. You might find it a bit difficult at first but there are a few simple steps to make sure you can cook successfully. This essay is going to explain each stage of preparing dinner: choosing what to eat, cooking it and serving it up.

4) _Stick to Your Plan_

Once you start writing, _don't get carried away_, go off on a tangent and forget about your plan.

Have some discipline in the way you write — keep your points in a logical order and don't wander off the topic.

Write in paragraphs.

Try and write at least _two sides_.

5) _Make it Interesting_

Don't be obvious. Add in any little _details_ that will make it more interesting.

BLINDING

BORING

Choose what food you want to eat.

Decide what food you want to eat. Pasta is quick to cook and provides lots of carbohydrates. Roasted meat is really tasty but it takes longer.

This should all be meat and drink to you by now...

Examiners aren't (necessarily) nasty people — they just know what they like. This kind of essay should be coherent, logical and persuasive. Do it like that and they will _love_ you for it.

Make Sure Everyone Can Understand

It's no good if you're the <u>only</u> one that understands what you're writing about — you've got to make sure that <u>everyone</u> will be able to get their head round it. But that's probably obvious.

Think About Your Readers

You're supposed to be <u>explaining</u> something.

1) *Explain things which might be obvious to you, but not necessarily obvious to <u>other people</u>.*

   This is no good —

   > Get a plant and grow it.

   You need to explain what you mean —

   > Buy some seeds from a garden centre. Dig a small hole and put the seeds in the hole. Water the area regularly.

2) *Try to anticipate any <u>bias</u> your reader may have. Then try to <u>respond</u> to what they might be thinking. A <u>balanced</u> argument is more likely to persuade people than a ranting one.*

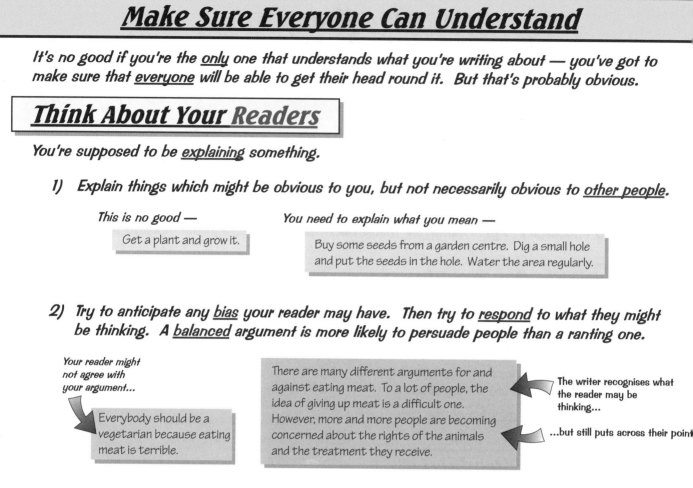

   Your reader might not agree with your argument...

   > Everybody should be a vegetarian because eating meat is terrible.

   > There are many different arguments for and against eating meat. To a lot of people, the idea of giving up meat is a difficult one. However, more and more people are becoming concerned about the rights of the animals and the treatment they receive.

   The writer recognises what the reader may be thinking...

   ...but still puts across their point

3) *Try to anticipate where the reader might get confused and make those bits especially <u>clear</u>.*

4) *Always <u>read over</u> what you've written. Think, "If I were reading this for the first time, would it make sense?" If not, you need to change it so that it does.*

Explain Unusual and Technical Language

1) *If you're writing about something you know well, it's easy to forget that your reader won't understand all the <u>technical words</u> you're using.*

2) *Your aim in all your writing should be to make it clear enough for anyone you can imagine reading it, to <u>understand</u> what you're saying.*

3) *Take care even when you're explaining something as <u>ordinary</u> as cooking dinner. You might think it's obvious what "boil the potatoes" means. But a reader who doesn't know about cooking needs you to explain that boil means, "put in boiling water."*

   The underlined words here are technical terms. They'll be understood by tennis experts...

   > The <u>serve-volley</u> game of Williams dominated Davenport's <u>ground strokes</u>. She repeatedly got to the <u>net</u> allowing her to take the first <u>set</u>, despite facing three break points in the <u>second game</u>.

   ...but others won't understand and will get confused.

But it all made perfect sense to me...

Burble, jabber, wibber, phtang... See how that technical jargon got you all confused — well, it's the same in the exam. But explain the tricky stuff properly, and you'll get more lovely, lovely marks.

Finishing Off Your Essay

At the end of your essay you need to tie up what you've been saying...

Finish Your Essay with a Conclusion

Before you start your conclusion look back at the <u>introduction</u>. Make sure that your conclusion agrees with the introduction. This will make the examiner feel as if the essay's a <u>complete package</u>, not just some random thoughts strung together.

Your conclusion should:

1 *Remind the reader about the <u>most important facts and ideas</u> in your essay.*

2 *<u>Give your opinion</u> on the topic you've been writing about.*

1 This bit reminds the reader about the main facts covered in the essay — how to get water, food, fire and shelter.

I hope you never are stranded on a desert island, but if it *does* happen remember that following these steps will massively increase your chances of survival: find water, find food, and then make a fire and shelter. Following these steps ensures you have the basic essentials for life. It will also make you feel more confident, and confidence is as much a key to survival as water, food, fire or shelter.

2 The final sentence has got an opinion about the facts in the essay.

You Must Check What You've Written

Once you've got a conclusion, go back over the whole essay and <u>check</u> these points:

Have you written a clear introduction which explains what the essay is about? ☐

Have you added some interesting and colourful details? ☐

Have you thought about your reader — where they might be confused or might disagree with what you've said? ☐

Have you explained all the technical terms you've used? ☐

As far as you can tell, is all the spelling and punctuation OK? ☐

1) If your answer to any of these questions is 'no', then do something about it.

2) There isn't much you can do if there are just 15 seconds to go — but five minutes is enough to <u>make a difference</u>. That's why it's so important to leave time for checking.

3) If you want to <u>add</u> anything, put a star (*) where you want the extra words to go and write them as clearly as you can in the margin.

4) If you want to <u>get rid</u> of anything, just cross it out. Don't scribble all over it.

I can hear a fat lady warming up right now...

The conclusion is your chance to hammer home what you've been talking about, and finish things off just nice. Just think how annoying it gets when something's unfinished and you don't know w...

Revision Summary

It's definitely pretty tricky to figure out the subtle differences between 'informing', 'explaining', and 'describing', but it *is* important for you to know what those differences are.
The main thing is that you're trying to give information to the reader. Otherwise, the basic rules for writing this essay are the same as for any other one. You've got to think about who you're writing for, and how to keep your writing lively, engaging and believable. So run through these questions and make sure that you've got all this knowledge locked up safe in the old noggin. You'll be thankful for it, come exam time...

1) Explain what is meant by each of these essay instructions in turn —
   a)   inform
   b)   explain
   c)   describe

2) Pick out the key words in these questions and say what you think the question is asking —
   a)   Explain some reasons for the use of speed cameras by police.
   b)   Write an article describing an ideal profession. The job could be real or imaginary.
   c)   Write an informative article for parents about music and the teenagers of today.

3) When choosing a topic to write on, why is it important to choose one that you know a lot about?

4) Explain what a good essay plan should achieve.

5) Why should you use lots of interesting details in your essay?

6) Which of these is the better explanation? Explain why.
   a)   Feed your dog some food.
   b)   You must feed your dog the right amount for its size. You can find out what this is from your vet or from books on your dog's breed.

7) Why do you think a balanced argument is more likely to persuade people than a ranting one?

8) Which of these descriptions is more suited to an essay? Why?
   a)   "Pilots should be able to deploy the chute, now fitted to all Cirrus SR20 light aircraft for test purposes, and float the entire bird to safety from 1000m high over Lexington, Ky."
   b)   "A new type of emergency parachute for aircraft is being tested in Kentucky."

9) Do you think you should refrain from using particularly difftastical technical verbiage? Why?

10) Why do you need to think about how the reader will react at all?

11) What's the point of writing a conclusion?

12) Explain what makes a really good conclusion.

13) Write down all the things you need to check for at the end of the exam.

14) Explain why it's important to leave yourself time at the end to go over your essay.

Starting Your Writing

Ah, this section is a great one. In fact it probably makes my Top 10 Sections In This Book. It's full of useful hints and ideas for writing your own stories — something most people find really scary.

Use What You Know to Get Ideas

You'll need a plot — a basic outline of what happens in your story.
You'll also need some main characters.
Start off by scribbling down some ideas. You could:

1) Write about something you're interested in. If you already know stuff about it, your story will be more realistic and it'll be easier to give lots of detail.

> If you know loads about science fiction, base your story in outer space. If you're into ballet then write about a dance class.

2) Write about something that's happened to you. It'll be easier for you, and your story will seem more life-like and genuine to the reader.

> If you saw a solar eclipse or won a donkey race, write about that.

Get Your Story Straight Before You Start Writing

Once you've got a rough idea of what's going to happen you need to plan your structure.
Write a brief synopsis of your story — a breakdown of the plot.

Beginning 1) Start by introducing your key characters. What do they want to achieve, and what obstacles stand in their way?

> A lot of stories are about conflict or struggle to achieve something. That's because characters have different motives — they have to compete or clash to get what they want.

Build-up 2) What's going to happen — how will you build up to the climax of your story?

> Give your characters a challenge. There has to be uncertainty or an element of risk to make it exciting.

Climax 3) Bring the action to a head. The main event or turning point should happen now.

> You need to build up the suspense and keep your reader guessing, up until this point. Otherwise the story will be boring.

Ending 4) Be sure that your conclusion makes some kind of point. Don't just tail off — you must tie up all loose ends.

> You could give it a moral, so that the characters learn something. Or you could give the story an unexpected twist.

Give it Bags of Style and Substance

To impress the people giving out those C - A* marks, you need to show you can write with imagination and flair. Check that your story has these things:

1) An entertaining plot that says something — there must be some point to it.

2) A clear structure — a beginning, middle and end that flow fluently together.

3) A variety of styles — different sentence lengths and structures, and interesting vocabulary.

4) Grammatically correct sentence- and paragraph-structure, punctuation and spelling.

5) It does what it's supposed to do. It must be written in a style that suits the audience it's aimed at.

My story's all wonky — there's a twist in the tail...

Don't panic about starting your writing. This section will show you how to turn a simple idea into a great story.   You still look a bit flustered.   Just try to r e l a x — it's going to be OK.

Say What Happened

Welcome to Page 48, Say What Happened, which is a smashing little page with some splendid advice and great examples. Well, I hope you enjoy it...

Tell Your Reader What Happened and do it Clearly

1) Your story needs to have a good <u>structure</u>. An epic adventure with hundreds of characters and loads of action is no good if your reader can't follow what's going on.

2) Everything you write should be <u>relevant</u> to the plot— in other words, leave out anything that's boring or doesn't need to be there.

Alfie likes star gazing, but he doesn't believe in UFO's.

He is planning to go camping in the forest.

ALFIE'S ALIEN ADVENTURE

Leave these bits out — they don't help the story.

Alfie always has boiled egg and soldiers for breakfast.

His sister's name is Edna.

Keep these bits — they're exactly what you need to tell the story.

Think About What Order it Should All Be In

1) You have to choose an <u>order</u> to tell your story in, that makes it interesting, and that gets the key points of your plot across in an entertaining way.

2) It's best to start with something <u>unusual</u> or exciting. Just writing a list of events in the order they would've happened can be pretty dull. Open with something that makes your reader curious.

> You could have a character frantically running — this'll get your reader wondering why.

3) As long as you <u>stick to the plot</u>, you can use any order you like.

> Your character could be very old at the start of the story, then they could talk about events that happened when they were young.

4) Just be sure to keep it <u>relevant</u>. Pretty obvious, but if you talk about details or bring in a character, make sure there's some point to it — that it's related to the story.

Make the Important Parts Really Stand Out

You have to make sure your reader really <u>understands</u> which bits are important. It's not enough to write long list of facts and events — that's boring. You need to add <u>details</u> and <u>vary your style</u>. Instead of just saying that a character is grumpy, explain why they're like that and what reaction other people have to them, like this:

> As he brushed the crumbs off his lap, Roger looked up and noticed that his sister had begun to sulk. He was used to this, because she had been grumpy ever since she was a baby. Even then she would spit her dummy across the room and scream at the top of her lungs.

Explain why what you're describing, matters:

1) Who cares about it?
2) What effect does it have on your characters?
3) How does it influence what happens?

> If your character is going to run a race, make it clear just how much they want to win and how nervous they are.

Give your readers structure — or they might lose the plot...

The examiner will notice if your story doesn't make sense or has irrelevant bits, and you'll lose marks. Emphasise important events by going into detail and using different styles.

Go Into Detail

Yes, English examiners _just love_ detail. It brings characters to _life_ and makes things more _interesting_. If you spent a whole day _shoving_ detail into examiners' mouths, they'd still be hungry at the end.

Always Say Where it Happened

1) You have to make sure you're really _specific_ — so the reader always knows exactly where the action is taking place. Then they can create a picture of what's happening, in their heads.

2) Make sure you keep it up _the whole way through_. This means more than just saying what town the story happened in. What was the house and the room like? Be as clear as possible — down to the last detail.

> Sam lived with her mum in Chorlton, Manchester.

→

> Sam lived in Chorlton, Manchester with her mum and brother. She spent most of her time playing the guitar in her bedroom, which was a tiny attic right at the top of the house. It was a damp, musty place, and she could often hear rats scuttling under the floorboards.

Think About Each of the Senses When You Write

Clearly you can't use every single one all the time — that would get boring and be far too silly. But think about each of the senses as you write and use them to make your story _sensational_:

Sight How things looked...	 **Sound** How things sounded...	**Smell** How things smelled...	 **Taste** How things tasted...	**Touch** How things felt...
The wall crumbled away to reveal a small tunnel with moss-covered walls winding into the distance.	Sam heard a faint, dripping sound echoing from somewhere deep inside the cave.	As she approached the door, a pungent smell like rotting vegetables suddenly filled her nostrils.	The broth tasted salty and strange. It was probably the worst thing she had ever eaten.	There was a sharp crunch under her foot. It felt like the shell of a snail or some other small creature cracking.

Think About the Characters' Thoughts And Feelings

The examiner will be impressed if you _get inside the characters' heads_. What are they thinking about? What motivates them? And how do they feel about the things that happen to them? A good way of showing this, is to write a section that is an _interior monologue_ — this means writing down the thoughts the characters are having, just as if they were speaking them out loud.

> Emily stood by her window, getting ready to lower a basket of treats from her bedroom to children in the street below.
> "I must remember not to lean out too far," she thought to herself, "as I am so nervous of being seen by strangers. I hope the children enjoy the treats, and let me draw the basket up again without any trouble."

◄ _This paragraph just shows Emily's thoughts._

This is a simple but effective trick. It puts the reader into the character's shoes — so they feel closer to them, as though they can _understand_ their feelings.

Bring your feelings into it — you know it makes sense...

"Mrs Chalice was looking so lovely today," he thought to himself, "but she could never like me. Could she? Perhaps if I changed my wig... Oh, what am I doing? Where am I? Day-dreaming again. Oh, I was going to write a tip about describing senses because that helps to bring stories to life. Oops."

Pace and Style

Writing at the same pace all the time can make for a dull read — like reading the diary of a three-toed sloth. You'll get more marks if you vary the pace and style to keep it interesting.

Vary The Pace To Make It More Interesting

You can *change the pace* — by switching between long, descriptive sentences and shorter, explanatory ones. The trick is to adjust the pace according to the mood of what is happening at that point in your story.

These sentences are short. They sound slower.

> It was Ahab's turn to keep watch. All his shipmates were gently nodding off to sleep. Even the waves seemed to nod slowly as if in a trance. Out of nowhere a gigantic sperm whale surfaced right by the boat, blowing out a thousand bubbles, and everyone woke up and shouted, clutching at the rails for safety.

This sentence is longer. It speeds up, and ends up sounding more energetic.

Of course, short sentences don't always have to slow the pace down. Sometimes they can be *short* and *punchy* to describe action scenes. You just have to make them as effective as you can.

> He saw me and yelled. I turned and ran. I was scared. I didn't see the step. I hit the deck. That's all I know.

Write Good Descriptions Using Images

Give *specific details* that set the scene for the reader, and help emphasise the important points.

Use *inventive images* to get the reader to conjure up a mental picture of what's happening — it makes them feel more involved.

This...

> Billie Holiday was a good singer.

...is not as effective as this.

> When Billie Holiday sang, it was like listening to her heart pouring out of her mouth. She sang with her entire body and soul, and put enough emotional force into her singing to make you want to cry.

Think About Shifting Perspectives

Perspective is the way you look at a situation — it's your point of view. Switching between perspectives is another effect that'll make your story more interesting to read — and it'll get you those top marks.

This could mean writing from *one character's perspective*, then switching to that of another.

> Billy's eyes widened as James took him by the arm and led him aside. He couldn't believe that his old friend looked so different.
> "It's been a long time, but you haven't changed a bit," said James, "Come with me and I'll explain everything."

Or it could mean writing about a character's perspective *a long time ago*, then commenting on their feelings today.

> It was thirty years since they had last seen each other. In those days James had followed Billy's lead as he caused chaos in school and wreaked havoc all over the town. Now as they made their way to the lake, Billy began to suspect that his friend would be taking charge from now on.

Pace yourself Ahab — we've a little whale to go yet...

It's vital to vary the pace in your story to keep the reader interested. You really have to think hard and not let the story get dull and go on and on and on and on and on and on and zZzzZZZz...

Finishing Your Essay

Examiners are complete suckers for a good ending. Your conclusion should make a point, have a twist or have some kind of moral. And then of course it's time to check it over.

Finish With A Conclusion

1) You need a paragraph at the end of your story that rounds up the plot nicely — it needs to <u>tie up all the loose ends</u>. There's nothing more frustrating than a story that leaves the reader hanging.

So <u>don't</u> end it with:

"Then I woke up — it had all been a dream."

2) The very <u>last line</u> is important — it needs to be written clearly and cleverly, so that it <u>sums up</u> the story for the reader and leaves them happy.

"Though life would never be the same again, he was glad to be home."

3) For the best marks, aim for the unexpected — finishing your story with a <u>twist</u> will really impress.

Drop a hint earlier on in the plot, then you can refer back to it later.

4) Another good device is to give your plot a <u>moral</u> — so that the story proves a point.

Think of the morals in different fairy tales — you could borrow one of these for your plot.

Keep Re-drafting — Until It's Just Right

1) <u>Edit</u> what you've written when you've finished your first draft.
2) Take time to tweak your story to get it as near-to-perfect as possible.
3) <u>Read</u> each paragraph through carefully and <u>underline</u> the bits you could improve on:

- *Could you go into more detail or change the wording to make yourself clearer?*
- *Is there a better word you could find to describe something?*
- *Have you repeated or over-used words or expressions?*

Check Your Grammar and Presentation Carefully

Think you've finished editing it? Then you need to read through the whole thing at least <u>two more times</u>.

1) Check that your <u>sentence formation</u> is accurate and correct.
2) Check that you've <u>spelt</u> all those interesting and unusual words right.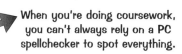

When you're doing coursework, you can't always rely on a **PC** spellchecker to spot everything.

3) Check that your <u>punctuation</u> is sound.
4) Check that you've got your <u>paragraphs</u> sorted and they flow nicely.

Finally, have a think about the <u>title</u> of the story. Is is snappy, is it clever? It should tell the reader something about your tale — but at the same time keep them guessing as to exactly what's coming...

And so I conclude that conclusions are conclusive. Maybe...

And that's it. The end of another wonderful section. So, how are you feeling? Inspired? No? Confident about writing your own stories now? No? Bored? Yes? Me too. I'm going home.

Revision Summary

Loads of people get really worried over this original writing bit — they think creative writing is something you can either just "do" or you can't. Well that's rubbish, and that's what this section is all about. You just need to learn the tricks of the trade that make stories seem really interesting and clever. And this is something that you can do without too much hassle for GCSE.

So make sure you go through every single one of these questions and examples, and you'll see just how easy it can be to do this 'original writing' malarky. Even for the born physicists among you...

1) Why should you write about things you're interested in and already know about?

2) For each of the following parts of a story, explain what each one should do —
    a) Beginning
    b) Build-up
    c) Climax
    d) Ending

3) Write out five things your story needs to have, to make the reader super-impressed.

4) Which of the following pieces of information could be used to put together a story? Say why you selected those particular bits and left the others out.
    a) Jess lives in Bristol
    b) Jess loves wearing spangly bracelets and dancing
    c) Jess's birthday is in November
    d) Jess once got abducted by alien Lizard creatures in her lounge
    e) Jess likes cheese

5) Explain why it's important to tell your story in an unusual or interesting order.

6) How can you make the really important bits of your story stand out to the reader?

7) a) Write a <u>good</u> and a <u>bad</u> description of someone's face (a few sentences is fine).
    b) Explain why one is better than the other.

8) Give an example of how each of the five senses might be used in a short story.

9) What is an 'interior monologue' and why should you use one?

10) Explain what is meant by the term 'perspective' and why you need to think about it when writing.

11) Let's say you've been abducted by aliens.
    a) Write a really dull paragraph about your abduction.
    b) Write a more interesting paragraph about your abduction (tips on p.50).
    c) Explain how you tried to make your second paragraph more interesting than the first one.

12) Why is a conclusion important in an original writing essay?

13) What should you check for, once you've finished?

Reading The Question

Non-fiction and media — <u>*barrel of laughs*</u>, for sure. Anyway, it's pretty much <u>*the same*</u> as writing about <u>*fiction*</u>, except you have to be able to spot <u>*bias*</u> and distinguish between <u>*fact and opinion*</u>.

4 Things To Get You Marks in Media Questions

These are all things that the examiner wants to give you marks for:

1 *Showing that you've <u>understood</u> and thought about what's in the text.*

2 *Making <u>clear</u>, <u>logical points</u> that are backed up with <u>references</u> to the text.*

3 *Telling the difference between <u>fact and opinion</u> (and spotting bias).*

4 *Using <u>technical words</u> confidently and successfully in your writing.*

<u>*Don't panic*</u> — this section'll show you how to do all these things, and the examiner will have to give you more marks for doing them...

The main thing is to stay calm, and to try and focus. Above everything else you must write <u>*clearly*</u>.

Be Sure To Read the Question Before the Text

Look at the question <u>*before*</u> you start on the text — it'll tell you exactly what to look out for. Having an idea of what you're looking for will help to <u>*focus*</u> your reading.

Pick out the <u>key words</u> in each question. Underline them, so you can see at a glance what the main point of each one is.

2. (c) Explain, using your own words, the writer's <u>opinion</u> about the <u>decline of line dancing</u> in the <u>last 8 months</u>.

1. (a) Write down two <u>facts</u> about the <u>need for security</u> at the Reading Festival.

Think About How Much the Question is Worth

1) The questions are worth different amounts of marks, as well you know.

2) Spend a <u>shorter</u> time on the questions that are worth <u>less</u>.

3) Think about what the question is asking you to do. If it wants 5 examples of something, then try and find them <u>quickly</u>. If it only wants 2 examples, you'll have to go into more <u>detail</u>.

What's the question worth? — I'll give you £5, just don't tell Betty...

Examiners may be 9-foot purple monsters with eyes that shoot fire.... but they're quite cuddly if they get what they want. And <u>what they want</u> is for you to show you've <u>understood the text</u>.

Reading The Text And Making Notes

No one likes making notes — seems like a complete waste of time. Wrong! Wrong! Wrong! Notes can stop you rambling on like a rambly thing with a "How to Ramble" book in International Rambling Week.

Find the Bits that Answer the Question

1 *You've got 15 minutes at the start of the exam just for reading. Go through the text at least twice, slowly and clearly. You'll have read the question, so you should be able to pick out all the bits that are relevant to it.*

2 *Keep track of the argument. It helps to mark the key points, as shown below.*

3 *Think about the language and tone of the piece as well, and write down anything that occurs to you.*

1. (a) In your own words, explain the attitude of the article towards Ben Kilham's approach, as well as towards those who criticise him.

GENTLE BEN

Most bear rehabilitators minimize human contact with their charges. Not Ben Kilham. When a forester brought him two bears, Anakin and sister Yoda, the frostbitten cubs moved into Kilham's guest room. "The bond isn't that hard to establish," he says, "They'd do anything to manipulate me into caring for them," — even raking him with sharp claws. Fattened on sheep's milk and applesauce, the cubs were soon moved to an enclosure outside of town where their education began. Some experts fear that such close contact may create a high proportion of nuisance bears. However, only two of Kilham's cubs are known to have become problems, preferring bird feeders to wilder fare.

Key point — Ben Kilham's approach is different from that of other bear specialists.

Key point — Ben says it's easy to bond with bearcubs.

The cubs were moved to an outdoor enclosure quite quickly.

This backs up the first point — namely that Ben's approach is not typical, and it worries people.

Language — scientific, authoritative, credible. The first sentence is a really good example.

Tone — humourous end. People are afraid for their own safety, worried that bears will eat them. The ending sides with Ben, saying that the only problems his bears have caused are feeding at bird feeders.

Think About the Tone

The tone of the writing is tailored to specific audiences. Different types of writing will use different tones — mention the tone and you'll impress the examiner. But just because it sounds convincing, doesn't mean it is...

A passionate, personal tone is often used by politicians in political speeches.
— it helps give the impression they believe sincerely in the argument they are making.

Articles in professional journals often use an impersonal, academic tone.
— they want their arguments to appear to be well-grounded in fact and research.

If I said I was a little bear would you hold it against me...

The examiners want to know you've understood the text. Even when you're still picking points out, always make notes in your own words. The examiner will spot any kind of copying.

Writing Your Answer

Big thing here is <u>no waffle</u>. Don't bury the examiner under loads of <u>irrelevant details</u>.
Be <u>precise</u>. Say what you think. Tell them <u>why</u> you think it, BASED on what the <u>text</u> has said.

Start Your Answer Confidently

You've got to sound believable — ALWAYS use <u>impersonal language</u> (e.g. "It seems", not "I think").
Your <u>first line</u> should show the examiner that you know exactly what the question's asking.
Reword the question as a <u>statement</u>, and make certain you seem self-assured.

> 2. (b) How does the magazine 'Careless Talk Costs Lives' use images, as well as text, to communicate meaning?

As an opening line, this would be about as popular as a rat in a biscuit tin. All it does is repeat the question.

> 'Careless Talk Costs Lives' uses images and text to communicate with its audience.

This is much <u>better</u>.

> 'Careless Talk Costs Lives' communicates with its readers using images which explain and emphasise the points made in the text.

Don't Just Copy From the Text

The examiner wants to know that you've <u>thought about</u> the text, and not just looked at it.
You'll get no marks for copying the text. Try and find interesting ways to <u>rephrase</u> the key points.

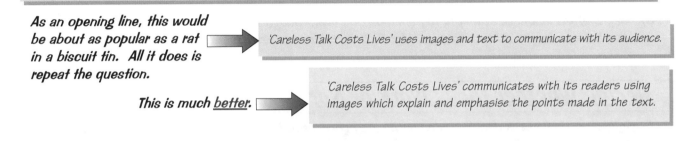

> *Rock'n'Roll eats its young — but sometimes they offer themselves up voluntarily. 'Manic Street Preachers' member Richey Edwards believed in the mythology of pop music; but rather than achieving some kind of transcendence, he met with a peculiar isolation.*

Awful — uses same words and is <u>dull</u>.

> The text says Richey Edwards believed in the mythology of pop music but was isolated.

Better — sounds <u>confident</u> and engaged with the text.

> The text says Richey Edwards remained isolated, despite his belief that pop music could reach beyond everyday life. It also suggests that he offered himself to this isolation, and brought it on himself.

Be Selective in Your Use of Detail

<u>Detail</u> is good — you need to <u>explain</u> what you're saying fully. BUT — don't overdo it. Select specific details that back up your point and help persuade the examiner — you'll get more marks.

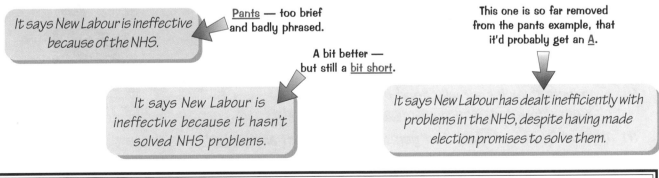

> It says New Labour is ineffective because of the NHS.

<u>Pants</u> — too brief and badly phrased.

> It says New Labour is ineffective because it hasn't solved NHS problems.

A bit better — but still a <u>bit short</u>.

This one is so far removed from the pants example, that it'd probably get an <u>A</u>.

> It says New Labour has dealt inefficiently with problems in the NHS, despite having made election promises to solve them.

Don't bury examiners with lots of detail — use soil...

OK, so you get the message — confident, uncluttered, own words... urghh... mmf... bored now.
Look, can't I just quietly nod off at the back here — I'm sure no one'll notice, pleeeeeeze...

Developing Your Answer

*This is the bit where you need to be <u>really critical</u> about the piece of writing. Pull it to <u>pieces</u> —
is there a <u>watertight argument</u>, or is the writer trying to pull the <u>wool</u> over your eyes...*

Don't Get Sucked in when there's No Evidence

1) <u>Back your statements up</u> with evidence to make them convincing
   — the more evidence used (from different sources), the more convincing it is.

2) Where there is no evidence, the writer will try to <u>persuade</u> you, using language.

3) Words to watch out for are POSSIBLY, ALLEGEDLY, APPARENTLY, SUPPOSEDLY, BELIEVE...

4) Don't get sucked in. Instead, write about the <u>language</u> in your answer.

5) Say that the language attempts to persuade you even though there are <u>no concrete facts</u>,
   and be sure to give a few examples. This will show the examiner that you can think for yourself.

Decide Whether Ideas Work or Not

*<u>Evaluating</u> an idea means deciding whether it's any good or not. BUT — the examiners don't want
your personal rant — they want to know why you think that. Back all your ideas up with <u>evidence</u>.*

What's the <u>point</u> being made?	Does the idea make <u>sense</u>?	Is there any <u>evidence</u>?
Sacco and Vanzetti were two poor Italians convicted of murder in the 1920s — the text says the judge and jury were biased against them.	Yes. People in U.S. at that time were scared of radical violence and the jury might have assumed they were guilty only because they were anarchists.	<u>WEAK SPOTS</u> 1) It's all "alleged" — not hard fact. 2) We don't know what the actual trial evidence against them was.

Think Beyond The Text

1) What questions do you have, about the idea, that are left <u>unanswered</u> by the source?

2) <u>Ask</u> questions — it'll show the examiner that you've really thought about it.

How could you <u>extend</u> the idea?

• Did the evidence at the trial, support a verdict of guilty or not guilty?

• Why were people scared of left-wing radicals?

• What was the reaction of the general American public to the verdict?

Compare and Contrast the Texts

1) Be sure to <u>compare</u> the bits of text you're given in
   the exam (as long as they've actually asked you to do that).

2) Examiners think it's a really good thing if you can
   pick out <u>differences</u> and <u>similarities</u> in texts.

3) Try and figure out which text you think works best and <u>say why</u>.

May as well do it this way. There's no evidence, and besides, everyone knows democracy doesn't really work anyway...

To get suckered or to not get suckered — that is the question...

*So — the crucial three questions are: 1) "What's the <u>point</u>?" 2) "Does the point <u>make sense</u>?"
3) "Is there any <u>evidence</u>?". Answer all of those in your essay, and you're well on the way.*

Writing About The Format of a Media Text

The <u>media</u> isn't just about making life <u>hell</u> for the <u>rich and famous</u> — nor is it just about <u>text</u>.
Newspapers, adverts, films, etc use a whole <u>stack of tricks</u> to make a point — layout, pictures, music...

Show You Can Understand Media Concepts

1) The examiner wants you to judge it as a media text, not just as any random exam text.
   You need to comment on the <u>format</u> — what it's trying to do and how well it works.

2) The <u>text</u> in the exam might be a magazine, radio and T.V. adverts, film scripts,
   scenes from films or other printed material like articles, press releases and fliers.

3) So, you have to think about other things besides the words — things like presentation,
   layout, graphics, structure, and actually commenting on the choice of the <u>medium</u> itself.

Think About What the Graphics are Trying to Do

If you get asked to comment on graphics, the
examiner expects you to be <u>clear and logical</u>.

> This just means that if you use
> <u>common sense</u> you'll get more marks.
> Literally just say what you see.

> Do they look good?
>
> Do they compliment the text?
>
> What do you think they're
> trying to achieve?

Mention The Layout

Different layouts are aimed at different
<u>audiences</u>. You should be able to work out
who the target audience is, for each text.

> This layout is <u>dull</u>. There's hardly any colour,
> the text is all of a similar size, and is justified,
> the header looks boring and the picture is
> formal. It's aimed at <u>professionals</u>.

> This layout is more <u>fun</u>. There's lots of
> colour, more space, the text size is varied, the
> picture and headers are more eye-catching
> and interesting. It's aimed at <u>young people</u>.

It Looks Great if You Can Use Technical Terms Appropriately

<u>CAPTION</u>: a short line to explain a picture.

<u>COLUMN</u>: newspapers and magazines
are normally laid out in columns.

<u>LEAD</u>: the main story on the front page.

<u>HEADLINE</u>: you know what a headline is.

<u>FEATURE</u>: longish story with more detail.

<u>EDITORIAL</u>: opinion column stating
newspaper's opinion.

<u>HUMAN INTEREST STORY</u>: focuses on
a personal story — often sentimental.

How to succeed in media — No. 1: move to London...

Well, after that page you should be able to sit down and watch your favourite TV programme and
read your favourite magazine, and scientifically spot all the "media tricks" they use to manipulate
you, without any of that "enjoyment" nonsense getting in the way. Hmmm...

Revision Summary

Media texts can be a bit tricky to wrap your head around (like a cat round a tin opener), but that's only because of one key element — you have to appreciate that they can rarely be trusted. Once you've realised that, and you approach every media text you read with a healthy dose of cynicism, you really will be well on the way to being able to answer these questions successfully. When you know that they're mostly just trying to influence you or sell you stuff, it gets easier to recognise the little tricks they have up their sleeves.

You know the drill, anyway. If you can get through these questions okay, you'll be just about ready to take on the world...

1) Name 4 things the examiners will definitely give you marks for.

2) Why should you read the question before the text?

3) Is there any point in thinking about how many marks a question is worth? Why?

4) Explain why it's important to read through the question slowly and make a few notes before you start thinking about where to start your essay.

5) Your specialist subject is, oh, let's say — jam. Write one sentence on 'jam' as an example of each of the following tones —
   a)   a passionate, personal tone
   b)   an impersonal, academic tone
   c)   an amused tone

6) What kind of initial impression do you want the introduction to your answer to make on the examiner?

7) Why do you think that simply copying from the text doesn't get you any marks?

8) "The Theory of Evolution is nonsense." — What is wrong with the way this is argued?

9) Why do you need to look for hard evidence that backs up the writer's opinions, in media texts?

10) Explain why you think examiners give out good marks when students show they can criticise a media text, and can say whether the ideas in it make sense or not.

11) What's the point of trying to think of questions that are left unanswered by the text?

12) Why is it important to think about what kind of media text it is (e.g. article, review, flier etc...)?

13) Is the layout important to consider in a media text? Why?

14) Briefly describe an example of each of the following (you can do a diagram if you fancy it) —
   a)   good use of graphics on a newsletter aimed at teenagers.
   b)   bad use of graphics on a newsletter aimed at teenagers.

15) Write a brief description of each of the following terms —
   a)   caption
   b)   column
   c)   lead
   d)   headline
   e)   feature
   f)   editorial
   g)   human interest story

Make Your Writing Clear To Read

Right then, my little bundles of joy... this book has been way too interesting so far.
What we could really do with now is something <u>dull</u> — yep... grammar... that should be fine.

Writing Properly Gets You a Better Grade

> To get an A or A* you have to:
>
> * get all your spellings right
> * get all your punctuation right
> * write sentences which are grammatically correct <u>and</u> varied
> * write in clear, linked paragraphs

Even if you're not aiming for an A you've <u>got</u> to get your spelling, punctuation, grammar and paragraphs sorted. The examiner will rob you of the marks you deserve if you make mistakes in basic language and grammar.

Writing Properly Makes Your Work Easier to Read

The four boxes below are the only bit of this book that you <u>don't</u> need to learn.
This stuff is just to prove that you've got to get your language and grammar spot-on.

This is <u>why</u> the examiners want you to be good at spelling, punctuation, grammar and paragraphs:

Spelling
If you don't spell words correctly then people won't even begin to know what you're trying to write.
Bad spelling can really distract readers.

Punctuation
Using correct punctuation makes your writing punchier.
Punctuation breaks sentences up into little bits so it's easier to make sense of them.

Grammar
Structuring sentences well means that no-one can get the wrong end of the stick.
It makes your writing varied and easier to read.

Paragraphs
Paragraphs make writing easier to read by dividing it into chunks.
Paragraphs show where you're starting on a new idea.

OK — now back to the learning...

Always Check For Stupid Mistakes

1) Getting this stuff right comes easily to some people.

2) For the rest of us it's tricky. The first thing to do is learn the rules in this section and use them when you're <u>actually writing</u>.

3) The second thing to do is to get into the habit of <u>checking</u> your work. If you check your work you can find the glaringly obvious mistakes and <u>correct</u> them.

Writing and speaking bad English won't get you nowhere...

It's true. I can't stand people what can't speak and write proper.

Standard English

You'll lose marks if you write as though you're talking to your mates. That's because examiners prefer to read Standard English. And also because they're not really interested in last night's telly.

Use Standard English

1) Everyone in Britain uses <u>different versions</u> of English — with different local words that can be difficult to understand.

Oooarr, get orf my laand!

2) <u>Standard English</u> is formal English. The point is that it avoids any local dialect words and helps people all over the country to understand each other.

Mad fur it aye our kid!

3) And more importantly, it's what the examiners want you to use.

Use Vocab and Grammar With Care

Using Standard English means following some <u>simple rules</u>.

1) Avoid writing as you'd speak, e.g. putting, 'like' or 'ok' after sentences.

2) Don't use slang or local dialect words that some people might not <u>understand</u>.

3) Don't use <u>clichés</u> (corny phrases that people use all the time), e.g. 'at the end of the day'. They're very boring and won't get you any marks.

4) Standard English means using the <u>correct</u> forms of words with correct spelling and grammar — so make sure you learn this whole section really well.

Avoid these Common Mistakes

Follow these <u>rules</u> in the exam — otherwise it could push you down a whole grade.

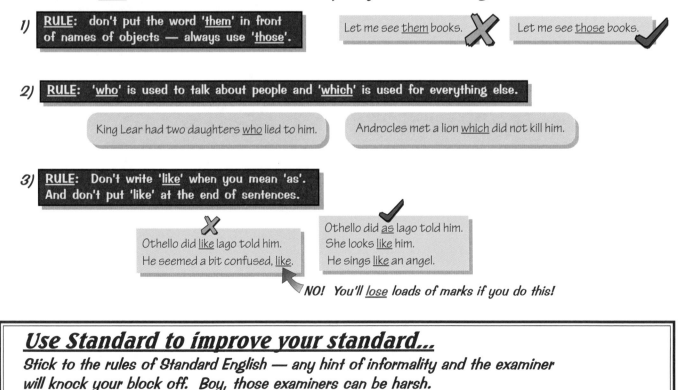

1) **RULE:** don't put the word '<u>them</u>' in front of names of objects — always use '<u>those</u>'.

Let me see <u>them</u> books. ✗   Let me see <u>those</u> books. ✓

2) **RULE:** '<u>who</u>' is used to talk about people and '<u>which</u>' is used for everything else.

King Lear had two daughters <u>who</u> lied to him.   Androcles met a lion <u>which</u> did not kill him.

3) **RULE:** Don't write '<u>like</u>' when you mean 'as'. And don't put 'like' at the end of sentences.

✗ Othello did <u>like</u> Iago told him.
He seemed a bit confused, <u>like</u>.

✓ Othello did <u>as</u> Iago told him.
She looks <u>like</u> him.
He sings <u>like</u> an angel.

NO! You'll <u>lose</u> loads of marks if you do this!

Use Standard to improve your standard...

Stick to the rules of Standard English — any hint of informality and the examiner will knock your block off. Boy, those examiners can be harsh.

Punctuation

Punctuation means all the dots, commas and other symbols that you need to put in your writing. And it's not just to make your essays look pretty — it's there for a reason. So read on...

Use Capital Letters and Full Stops Properly

Pretty basic stuff — you NEED to use them correctly to get beyond a grade F.

1) Always start sentences with a _capital letter_...

2) ...and always end sentences with a _full stop_.

3) Full stops mark a definite _pause_ before the next sentence starts.

Use Commas to Put Pauses in Sentences

You need to use commas to get decent marks.
Learn the _3 rules_ below to improve your chances of a good grade, instantly.

1) Commas are used to _separate_ words or groups of words so that the meaning is made clear.

> In the valley below, the villages all seemed very small.

Without the comma, the sentence would say 'in the valley below the villages'.

2) Commas are also used to break things up in a _list_:

> I bought onions, mushrooms, peppers and pasta.

3) You need to use commas to add _something extra_ to sentences:

> The twins, who had their blue wigs on, were eating grass.

The sentence would still work without the bit in the middle.

Semicolons Link Sentences

1) Semicolons _link_ sentences to make one big sentence.

2) The two parts on either side of the semicolon must be _equally important_.

> It's getting late; we won't get there on time.

Both parts are equally important.

Semicolons and colons are tricky, so don't use them unless you're 100% sure how they work. BUT do use them (when appropriate) if you want to get a grade A or B.

Colons Divide Sentences

1) Colons are used to _divide_ sentences if the second half explains the first half:

> The ballroom had become very empty: most of the guests had left.

2) You should _only_ use a colon if the first part leads on to the second part.

3) Colons can also be used to introduce _lists_.

> You will need: an apple, wool, and glue.

Ellipses and Dashes Mark a Long... Pause

1) Ellipses are just '_dot dot dot_' to you and me.

2) Ellipses mark a _really long pause_...even longer than a full stop.

3) Dashes do basically the same thing — and they _separate_ parts of a sentence nicely.

4) Dashes and ellipses are quite _informal_ so only use them in original writing.

You NEED to learn this stuff on punctuation — full stop...

lordy lordy just think how hard it would be to read something without punctuation it would drive you up the wall and it's the same for the examiners they can't stand it at all so use it I tell you

Apostrophes

Apostrophes are something everybody gets wrong. Well not everybody, obviously, but my greengrocer does. Anyway, you need to get them figured out or you won't get above a C.

You've Got to Add 's to Show Who Owns Something

The dog belongs to Montel so you add an <u>apostrophe</u> + '<u>s</u>' to the name of the owner.

Montel's dog is less scary now.

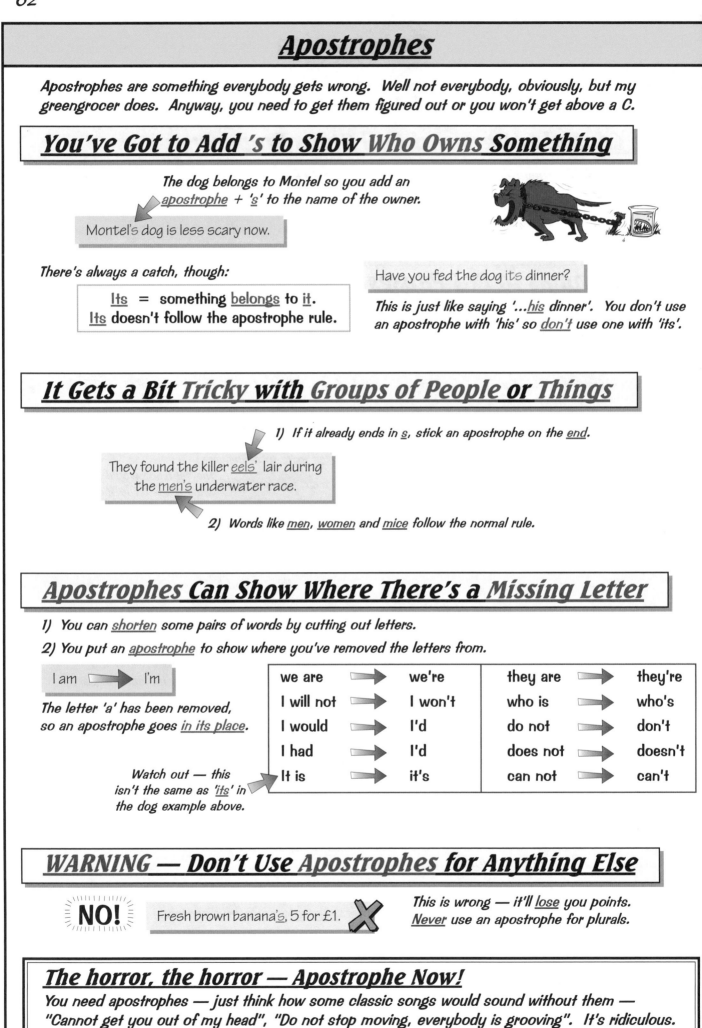

There's always a catch, though:

> <u>Its</u> = something <u>belongs</u> to <u>it</u>.
> <u>Its</u> doesn't follow the apostrophe rule.

Have you fed the dog its dinner?

This is just like saying '...<u>his</u> dinner'. You don't use an apostrophe with 'his' so <u>don't</u> use one with 'its'.

It Gets a Bit Tricky with Groups of People or Things

1) If it already ends in <u>s</u>, stick an apostrophe on the <u>end</u>.

They found the killer <u>eels'</u> lair during the <u>men's</u> underwater race.

2) Words like <u>men</u>, <u>women</u> and <u>mice</u> follow the normal rule.

Apostrophes Can Show Where There's a Missing Letter

1) You can <u>shorten</u> some pairs of words by cutting out letters.

2) You put an <u>apostrophe</u> to show where you've removed the letters from.

I am ➡ I'm

The letter 'a' has been removed, so an apostrophe goes <u>in its place</u>.

Watch out — this isn't the same as '<u>its</u>' in the dog example above.

we are ➡ we're		they are ➡ they're
I will not ➡ I won't		who is ➡ who's
I would ➡ I'd		do not ➡ don't
I had ➡ I'd		does not ➡ doesn't
It is ➡ it's		can not ➡ can't

WARNING — Don't Use Apostrophes for Anything Else

NO!

Fresh brown banana<u>'s</u>, 5 for £1. ✗

This is wrong — it'll <u>lose</u> you points. <u>Never</u> use an apostrophe for plurals.

The horror, the horror — Apostrophe Now!

You need apostrophes — just think how some classic songs would sound without them — "Cannot get you out of my head", "Do not stop moving, everybody is grooving". It's ridiculous.

Speech Marks

I know, I know... I'm beginning to sound like a stuck record now.
But speech marks are yet another thing the examiner will be looking out for.

Speech Marks Show Someone's Actually Speaking

Start of
speech

End of
speech

"You're going to lose that pretty hat," said Bob.

These are the words Bob said
— they go in the quotation
marks.

Always Start Speech with a Capital Letter

"Let's have a game of pogo-stick golf," said Claude.

Here's the capital letter.

Doug asked, "Where's the nineteenth hole?"

The speech bit always has a capital letter —
even if it isn't at the start of the sentence.

End Speech with a Question Mark, Full Stop or Comma

"Who will fight me in a duel?" asked Louise.

Remember — spoken questions have
to have a QUESTION MARK.

Marco shouted, "I'm not afraid to fight."

This speech isn't a
question. It's got
to end with a full
stop instead.

"You're no match for me," replied Louise bravely.

This isn't a question either. The speech has
finished but the sentence hasn't — you need a
comma here.

The punctuation rules are exactly the same whether you're writing dialogue in a
story, or quoting from a poem in a literature essay. For more on quoting, see P. 5.

Unaccustomed as I am...

Actually remembering to use speech marks is easy enough — it's working out where all the
punctuation goes that's the problem. But it's not impossible, so stop bleating and learn the rules.

Negatives

I'll pass on some advice my granpappy gave to me — he sat me down on his knee one day and said, "Now don't you go using no double-negatives, you hear." My granpappy was a wise man.

'No' Isn't the Only Negative Word

1) <u>Negative</u> sentences are the opposite of positive sentences (duh).

2) The easiest way to make a phrase negative is to add '<u>no</u>' or '<u>not</u>'.

3) Words ending in <u>-n't</u> are also negative.

Positive sentence:	Negative sentence:
My aubergines are rotten.	My aubergines are not rotten.

Don't Use Double Negatives

I don't want no aubergine.	**REALLY MEANS**	I do want some aubergine.

> <u>Two negative words</u> in the same phrase will make it <u>positive</u>.
> You should use only <u>one negative</u> at a time.

1) The main thing to remember is that words ending in '<u>-n't</u>' are <u>negative</u>...

2) ...so you don't need to add '<u>no</u>' or '<u>not</u>'.

The Word None has Three Meanings

1) '<u>None</u>' is a word that can cause problems. As a <u>pronoun</u> it means 'not one' or 'not any':

"Did you see any film stars?" "We saw none."	"Have you got any aubergines?" "I'm afraid there are none left."

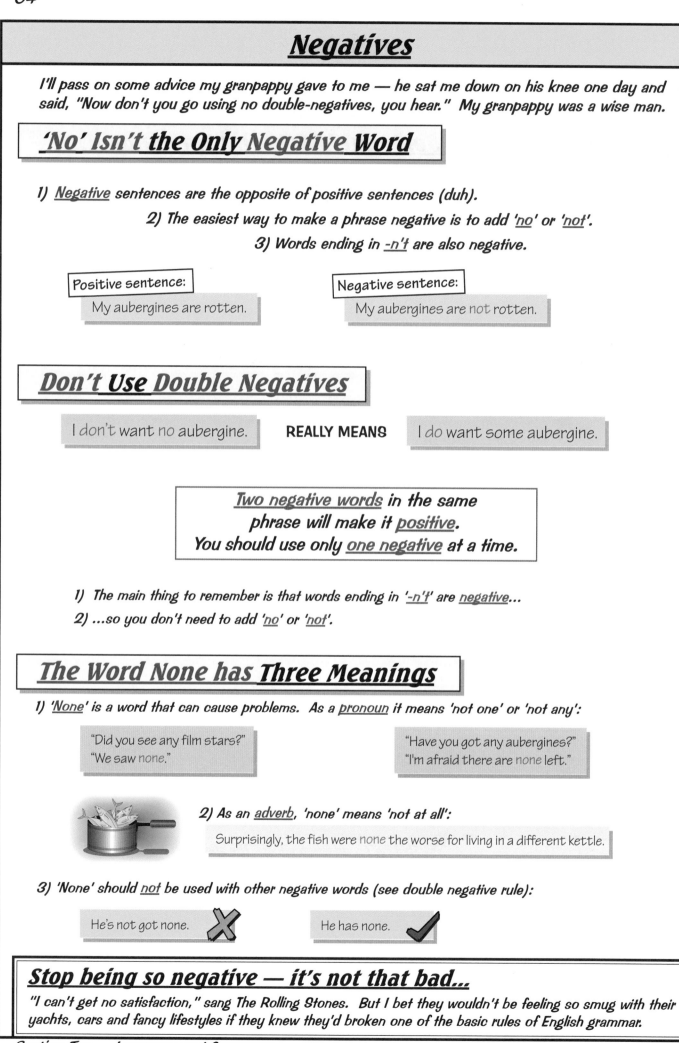

2) As an <u>adverb</u>, 'none' means 'not at all':

Surprisingly, the fish were none the worse for living in a different kettle.

3) 'None' should <u>not</u> be used with other negative words (see double negative rule):

He's not got none.	He has none.

Stop being so negative — it's not that bad...

"I can't get no satisfaction," sang The Rolling Stones. But I bet they wouldn't be feeling so smug with their yachts, cars and fancy lifestyles if they knew they'd broken one of the basic rules of English grammar.

Spelling

I knew an English-examiner once (actually, he smelt and wasn't very nice). He told me that the thing he hated most in the world was gravy. But he said he didn't like bad spelling either.

Some Words Sound the Same but have Several Spellings

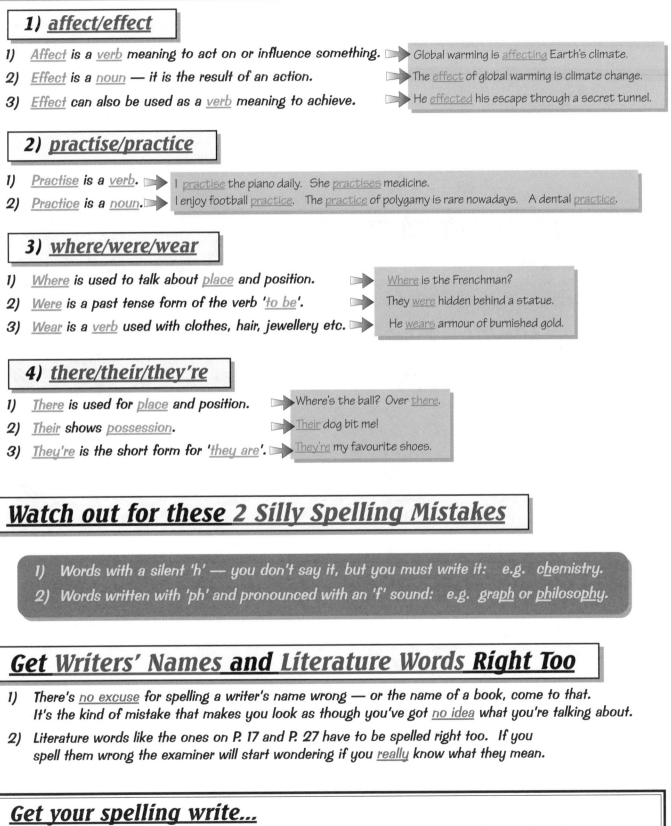

1) affect/effect

1) <u>Affect</u> is a <u>verb</u> meaning to act on or influence something. ➡ Global warming is <u>affecting</u> Earth's climate.

2) <u>Effect</u> is a <u>noun</u> — it is the result of an action. ➡ The <u>effect</u> of global warming is climate change.

3) <u>Effect</u> can also be used as a <u>verb</u> meaning to achieve. ➡ He <u>effected</u> his escape through a secret tunnel.

2) practise/practice

1) <u>Practise</u> is a <u>verb</u>. ➡ I <u>practise</u> the piano daily. She <u>practises</u> medicine.

2) <u>Practice</u> is a <u>noun</u>. ➡ I enjoy football <u>practice</u>. The <u>practice</u> of polygamy is rare nowadays. A dental <u>practice</u>.

3) where/were/wear

1) <u>Where</u> is used to talk about <u>place</u> and position. ➡ <u>Where</u> is the Frenchman?

2) <u>Were</u> is a past tense form of the verb '<u>to be</u>'. ➡ They <u>were</u> hidden behind a statue.

3) <u>Wear</u> is a <u>verb</u> used with clothes, hair, jewellery etc. ➡ He <u>wears</u> armour of burnished gold.

4) there/their/they're

1) <u>There</u> is used for <u>place</u> and position. ➡ Where's the ball? Over <u>there</u>.

2) <u>Their</u> shows <u>possession</u>. ➡ <u>Their</u> dog bit me!

3) <u>They're</u> is the short form for '<u>they are</u>'. ➡ <u>They're</u> my favourite shoes.

Watch out for these 2 Silly Spelling Mistakes

1) Words with a silent 'h' — you don't say it, but you must write it: e.g. <u>c</u>hemistry.

2) Words written with 'ph' and pronounced with an 'f' sound: e.g. <u>graph</u> or <u>philosophy</u>.

Get Writers' Names and Literature Words Right Too

1) There's <u>no excuse</u> for spelling a writer's name wrong — or the name of a book, come to that. It's the kind of mistake that makes you look as though you've got <u>no idea</u> what you're talking about.

2) Literature words like the ones on P. 17 and P. 27 have to be spelled right too. If you spell them wrong the examiner will start wondering if you <u>really</u> know what they mean.

Get your spelling write...

Spelling words right is pretty gosh-darn important. That's what I say. That's what the examiners say. And that's what Abraham Lincoln would say if he were alive today. (Possibly.)

Sentences

I have something earth-shattering to tell you. Get ready for this... it's going to change your life.
You need to check that your sentences make sense. That's it. Now go and have a lie down.

Every Sentence Needs a Verb

1) Verbs are '*doing*' words or '*being*' words...
2) ...and *every* sentence needs to have one.

They walk through the shopping centre.

Here's the action in this sentence
*— it's the '*doing*' word.*

Past tense

I was the world's first snail-tamer.

*These are both '*being*' words*
— but they're in different tenses.

I will be the world's first snail-tamer.

Future tense

Make Sure that Numbers Agree Too

The *verb ending* has to match whether the number of the subject is *singular* or *plural*.
When you're writing a verb in a sentence, say it out loud. Decide whether it sounds right or not.

OUCH! *This sounds wrong.*

Jill like mouse sandwiches. ✗

Much better — that sounds
right and it makes sense too.

Jill likes mouse sandwiches. ✓

NO!

The mice hates crusty bread. ✗

Phew — that's better.

The mice hate crusty bread. ✓

Don't Change Verb Tenses in Your Writing By Mistake

This is past tense.

Another past verb.

As they tried to get the sail up, they could hear
distant splashes — then they see a canoe.

This one's wrong — it's present
when it should be past.

Future tense? — you will be soon...

If you don't follow these three rules, then you're asking for trouble.
Worse than that... if you don't follow these three rules, you're mad.

> Remember to stick a
> verb in every sentence
> you write.

Sentences

Sentences have to make sense to get any grade above an F. But, to take you into the heady realm of Cs and above, you also need to think about how well your sentences flow together.

Vary the Style of your Sentences

To get grade C to A* you need to make your sentences _interesting_ to read, as well as clear.
There are easy ways of doing this:

1) Use _parallel structure_ — it basically means repeating words within a sentence.

The Spanish, French and Italians all have a snooze every afternoon. → The Spanish, the French and the Italians all have a snooze every afternoon.

Repeating '_the_' makes it sound loads better.

You can also use parallel structure to _remind_ the reader what you're _talking about_:

I used to write essays with ink, while now mustard is used. → I used to write essays in ink; now I write them in mustard.

The repetition of '_I write_' keeps the reader focused on the point of the sentence.

2) _Start_ your sentences in different ways:

There was a chill in the air as Jo walked towards the house. There was nobody around. There was a big oak door and Jo knocked on it. There was a scream from inside the house.

Boring — the word 'there' is repeated all the time.

This says the same things, but in a more interesting way.

There was a chill in the air as Jo walked towards the house. Nobody was around. Jo knocked on the big oak door. A scream came from inside the house.

3) Vary the _length_ of sentences. Mix together long and short sentences to make your essay more interesting to read — you'll get better marks for it.

The contrast of long and short sentences works well.

Cornwall is in trouble. The tourists flock to this lovely area every year, clogging up the road with slow-moving caravans and leaving behind piles of litter to endanger the local wildlife and pollute the sea. Something has to be done.

Chronological Order Makes Things Easy to Follow

Your sentences need to be in the right _order_ — if the examiner can't follow them easily you'll lose marks. _Chronological order_ (the order in which things happened) is the most logical order.

Harry went flying and landed in a silage pit. Unfortunately it was faster than him and, just before he reached the gate, it headbutted him with all its force. Harry turned to run as the angry bull careered towards him.

What's happening _isn't clear_, because the sentences aren't in chronological order.

The chronological order _should_ be:

1. Harry turned to run as the angry bull careered towards him. → 2. Unfortunately it was faster than he was, and just before he reached the gate, it headbutted him with all its force. → 3. Harry went flying and landed in a silage pit.

Parallel structure — repeating repeating words words...

Thinking about the style and order of your sentences is a good way of making your writing more sophisticated. Examiners like sophistication. That's why they all wear cravats and cummerbunds.

Writing Varied Sentences

Writing 'properly' isn't enough — your writing has to be interesting too, if you want to get a C or above. A good thing to do is to make sure you use lots of different words, e.g. wheelbarrow.

Use Different Words for the Same Thing

Don't fall into the trap of using the same word all the time — especially adjectives like "nice" or "weird". Examiners don't like it and you'll lose loads of marks.

DULL

I went to a nice Indian restaurant last night. The waiters were nice to us and the walls were painted in a nice shade of red. I had an onion bhaji to start with and it was really nice. Then I had a nice curry. After the meal the waiters brought us mints, which was nice of them.

It may be 'correctly' written, but it's not going to score you any points because it's so boring.

ACE

I went to a fantastic Indian restaurant last night. The waiters were friendly to us and the walls were painted in a lovely shade of red. I had an onion bhaji to start with and it was really tasty. Then I had a delicious curry. After the meal the waiters brought us mints, which was kind of them.

This is loads better. Using lots of different adjectives paints a more interesting picture — and you'll get loads more marks for it.

It's the same with verbs...

I ran to the post box with a letter, then I ran to the shop for some chocolate. After that I ran home so I wasn't late for tea.

I ran to the post box with a letter, then I hurried to the shop for some chocolate. Finally I raced home so I wasn't late for tea.

Fancy Words Impress the Examiner

Using different words is a good start. If you can use different and clever words, then you're laughing — they can really improve your grade.

United played badly on Saturday.

United played lamentably on Saturday.

The flooded pitch didn't help the standard of play.

The saturated pitch was detrimental to the standard of play.

The referee made some very stupid decisions.

The referee made some exceedingly moronic decisions.

You can't use long, fancy words all the time — that'd sound daft. But you'll get extra marks if you throw them in now and then. So remember this rule:

sporadically   endeavour   substitute   concise
Every now and then, try to replace a short and simple word with a long and clever one.
elementary   complex   intellectual

Use looooonnnggg wooooorrdddsssss...

Get a dictionary and learn some crazy new words, or sleep with one under your pillow and try to absorb the words as you sleep. It'll help you get loads more marks. (Except the pillow thing won't work.)

Writing Varied Sentences

I'll tell you where to find a couple more tricks that'll help win the examiner over.
But I can only whisper it. So come a bit closer... a bit closer... that's it... they're here on this page — where else would they be...

Describe Things by Comparing them to Other Things

Comparisons create interesting <u>visual images</u> for readers. It's good to use them instead of adjectives sometimes — variety is the source of extra marks as well as the spice of life, so they say.
There are <u>two</u> different ways of comparing:

1) Less than, more than, the least, the most...

Lisa's face went green.	Lisa's face went <u>more blotchy than</u> a dalmatian's.
It was very cold.	It was <u>colder than</u> an Arctic winter.
She was beautiful.	She was the <u>most beautiful</u> woman this side of Stockport.

When you're making a comparison, you must **EITHER** say "more ... than" or "the most...", **OR** you use the form of the word that ends in "er" or "est". You DON'T do BOTH.

WATCH OUT: You are the <u>most sporty</u> person I know. **NOT** the "most sportiest". Jenny is <u>prettier than</u> her sister. **NOT** "more prettier".

2) Use <u>similes</u> (say that one thing is <u>like</u> another). There are two ways of using similes...

① *The first is to take an adjective, think of a comparison, and then instead of using "more" and "than", you use "<u>as</u>" and "<u>as</u>".*

Beth felt <u>as</u> happy <u>as</u> a hippo in a mud pool.

② *The other way of saying one thing is like another is nice and simple — you use the word "<u>like</u>".*

I'd forgotten my gloves and soon my fingers were <u>like</u> blocks of ice.

It's OK to <u>exaggerate</u> when you make comparisons. It'd be pointless if you were totally accurate. You'd have to write things like "Jack was as tall as a six foot two inch tree" — no fun at all.

Use Metaphors

You use <u>metaphors</u> when you talk about one thing as if it <u>were</u> something else, rather than as if it were like something else. It's quite a sophisticated way of <u>livening up</u> your writing. You should use it if you're aiming for a C or above.

Leela cried so hard that a river flowed down her cheeks.

Wai Yin needed a glass of water — there was a desert in her mouth.

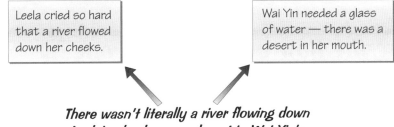

There wasn't literally a river flowing down Leela's cheeks, or a desert in Wai Yin's mouth, but the language creates a <u>strong visual image</u> and gets the point across well.

I've told you a million times — stop exaggerating...

Using similes and metaphors will make the examiners see your work as an oasis of loveliness in the lonely desert of tedious, unimaginative essays that they all too often have to mark.

Nouns, Verbs, Adverbs & Adjectives

"The poem is full of descriptive adverbs," sounds about five grades better than, "I like the words." So quit your whining and get on with learning what nouns, verbs and thingies are.

A Noun *is a* Person, Place *or* Thing

There are four kinds of noun:

Proper Names

Gloria, Tuesday, Texas

Proper names always have *capital letters*.

Groups of people or things

class, pack, squad

Names of things or places

hedge, hair, woman

These are just *everyday words*.

Words for ideas

truth, beauty, fear

You can't see, hear, or touch them — but they're still *nouns*.

Verbs *are* 'Doing' *or* 'Being' Words

'Doing' words

riding   thinks

ate   belches

'Doing' words tell you *what's happening* in a sentence. Don't always use the same ones — or the examiner will be bored and will give you bad marks.

'Being' words

Today was a good day.

I am happy.

'Being' words tell you how something *is* or *was* or *will be*.

Adjectives Describe Things *and* People

Global warming is bad.

Too boring — *zero marks alert*!

Global warming is a *serious* and very *worrying* issue.

Much better — the *adjectives* will help to impress the examiner.

Adverbs *Describe How an Action* is *Done*

The army retaliated, attacking the fortress.

Not much fun, this.

The army *promptly* retaliated, *viciously* attacking the fortress.

The *adverbs* make the sentence more *exciting* — which means more marks coming your way.

I always turn off the TV during the adverbs...

Use different verbs, adjectives and adverbs to spice up your writing. It'll get you more marks in the exam, and help to make you more attractive to the opposite sex*. *Well, it won't make you *less* attractive, anyway.

Revision Summary

There's quite a lot of stuff to take on board, here. Have a browse back over this section, and when you feel confident, try these questions. Nip back and check the ones you get wrong, then have another bash. It'll take a little while — but you need to be able to sail through the questions like a knife through butter...

1) What four things do you need to do in your writing to get an A or an A* grade?

2) When you have finished, why is it important to check through your writing?

3) Write a paragraph to show that you know what standard English is.
Jot down one example of standard English and one of non-standard English.

4) True or false: you should try to use dialect words, slang and clichés when writing in standard English.

5) Name three things you need to remember so that you don't make mistakes when writing standard English.

6) What are the three places where you can use commas?

7) What are semicolons used for?

8) What are colons used for?

9) What do ellipses and dashes do? And when should they be used?

10) Correct the mistakes in these sentences:
a) The hamster has looked very happy since I brushed it's coat.
b) Its nice to see a smile on its little face.

11) Cut out letters and replace them with apostrophes. The first one is done for you.
a) I will not = I won't   b) can not   c) I had   d) It is   e) they are

12) True or false: You should use apostrophes for plurals.

13) What should speech always start with when you're writing? And what should it end with?

14) What is a double negative and why are they bad?

15) Which of these statements is correct?
a) We where going to a fancy party.
b) I decided to wear my birthday suit.
c) I don't know were that idea came from.

16) What kind of word does every sentence need to have in it?

17) What is it important to remember about verb tenses when you are writing?

18) When you are writing, why would you use:
a) parallel structure?   b) sentences of different lengths?

19) What is chronological order? Why is it a good thing to stick to it?

20) True or false: Using different and fancy words will impress the examiner.

21) When you're writing, why is it good to make comparisons between things?

22) What are two ways of using similes?

23) What is figurative language? Why would you want to use it?

24) Name the four kinds of noun and give two examples of each.

25) What are verbs?

26) What do adjectives describe?

27) What do adverbs describe?

Speaking and Listening

For some lucky people, the speaking bit's great — but for everyone else it can be a nightmare.
It's much less scary if you've worked out what to say first — so treat this page like gold dust...

There are Three Main Categories of Practical Test

Any particular test you have to do will be assessed according to which <u>category</u> it is in.

Categories are:

> 1) explain – describe – narrate
> 2) explore – analyse – imagine
> 3) discuss – argue – persuade

A <u>debate</u> would be category 3.

Giving a <u>talk</u> or having a <u>discussion</u> could fit any category, depending on the subjects asked for.

Examiners are on the lookout for certain things in the Speaking tests.
You've got to do these things if you want to get the marks:

What you need to do for an A*:
Use standard English vocabulary and grammar.
Listen carefully to other people who are talking.
Express tricky ideas clearly.
Adapt your talk to the task and audience, and make it original and interesting.

Remember the CAP Rule When You Speak

Think about these things <u>before</u> you start any Speaking practical — <u>learn</u> and remember them.

1) **COURTESY** — Be <u>polite</u> at all times, especially when other people ask questions, or when they're doing their tests. If you're polite, they'll be on <u>your side</u> when you do your tests.

OI, YOU LOT! Shut up and listen to this!

2) **AUDIENCE** — Adapt your speech to the audience. You'll be speaking to a big group, so you'll have to keep people's attention. Tell a <u>joke</u>, or use a <u>visual aid</u> to make your talk more interesting.

3) **PURPOSE** — Get your information across in an <u>interesting</u> way, as <u>clearly</u> as possible. Just keep it short, clear and to the point.

REMEMBER: CAP (Courtesy, Audience, Purpose)

Don't worry about the Speaking Exam — it's all talk...

And at least it's only your best mark in each category that counts — you get more than one go.

Speaking and Listening

WAIT WAIT — don't turn over, I haven't finished yet! If you don't read this page, I'll... I'll...
...Well, it doesn't really matter what I'll do — but I guarantee you it won't be pleasant.

Use Standard English

Standard English isn't only useful when you're writing.

The examiner wants you to speak in standard English, so do it.
It doesn't mean you have to hide your accent — just speak clearly.

Don't use slang if you're giving a speech or a talk. You'll lose
marks. In a discussion it's OK to speak a bit more normally.

*For more on
Standard
English, take a
look at P. 60.*

Make Your Talk Clear

1) Don't mumble into your collar. Speak up and look around the room while you're talking.
   That way you can at least be sure everyone can hear you.

2) Give your talk a clear structure. Don't just ramble on through a fog of disconnected points.

> Work out the most important piece of
> information you have to communicate.
> Use that at the beginning of your talk
> — it'll get people interested.

> Don't repeat yourself. Once
> you've finished making a point
> then move on to the next point.

> Talk clearly and plainly. Long fancy
> words are useless if no-one
> understands what you're saying.

> Draw attention to the
> most important facts.
> Then the audience will
> remember them.

Writing notes will stop you from getting off the point of your talk.
Don't write out every single word you want to say — you'll end up reading out your notes.

Listen Carefully and Be Polite

Even when you're not talking, you're being assessed.
You've got to show you're following what other people say too.

1) Concentrate on what the other person is saying. That means you won't miss anything.

2) If you're unsure of a point they've made, politely ask for it to be repeated more clearly.

3) Don't interrupt speakers in mid-flow. Let them finish before you have your say.

4) Always respond constructively — talk about any good things that the other person said.

5) If you want to criticise, then be critical about their opinion, explaining why you think their
   argument is wrong. Never attack people personally — you'll lose marks in a practical test.

6) You've got to be sure that your own views make sense. Never criticise people
   if they are talking about subjects you don't understand. Ask them to explain.

You must speak properly — like what I does...

Mmmfff... well, only one more page to go, I suppose.

74

Having a Debate

You might have to take part in a debate in your Speaking test. AAARRGGGHHH.....
Don't worry — if you stick to the debating rules, you'll pick up the marks, no problem.

Debates Argue For and Against a Motion

The subject to be debated is called the motion. Debates are always structured the same way:

1) The Chairperson then opens the debate to the Floor, and anyone in the audience who wants to speak can put up their hand. The Chairperson can signal to them that they may speak.

2) All speakers address the Chairperson before they speak.
The Chairperson is the final authority while the debate is going on.

3) After a few minutes of Floor debate, the Chairperson asks the Opposer to sum up the case against the motion briefly. The Proposer then sums up quickly too.

4) The Chairperson takes a final vote from the audience — people can vote for the motion, against it or abstain (don't know) — if a majority supports the motion it is passed.

5) If the vote is tied, then the Chairperson has a casting vote — deciding who wins.

Prepare to Defend Your Corner

During a debate, the examiner will be watching to see how well you've prepared your case.

1) Research your case carefully — then you'll know the facts inside out.

2) Work with the other person in your team. The seconder should back up the other person, and make their argument seem even more convincing.

3) Keep to the point. You need people to remember exactly what your opinion is.

4) Use two or three strong arguments with your best point for a conclusion.

5) You're allowed to be one-sided here — but use facts to support your ideas.

6) Don't attack people personally. You won't get any marks for being a bully — you'll only get marks if you argue calmly and methodically.

Debates are like restaurants — there are lots of orders...

The key thing is: you don't need to win the debate. The examiners only care whether you can argue well. So make sure you learn all those tricky procedures and know what's going to happen.

Index

Index